Praise for *Influence and Impact*

"Berman and Bradt generously teach the reader how to apply well-tested coaching tools to being more influential and achieve impact at work. While previously available only to a privileged group of executives who can afford an expensive executive coach, these tools are now accessible to all. Working through the book leaves no room for feeling helpless or stuck."

Konstantin Korotov, Ph.D., Professor of Organizational Behavior, ESMT Berlin

"This remarkable book decodes how to lead with maximum impact by harnessing a laser focus on mission-critical business and cultural priorities. An indispensable and highly accessible reference, the coverage is broad, deep, and offers unique career insights and advice for those who are charged with leading others and transforming organizations."

John C. Scott, Chief Operating Officer, APTMetrics, Inc.

"Berman and Bradt are brilliant. They have decades of helping leaders crack the code on how to have Influence and Impact. How do leaders manage challenging situations? Read this book. No matter who you are you will find nuggets of pure gold that you will be able to put into practice, tomorrow."

Carol Kauffman, Ph.D., ABPP, Founder, Institute of Coaching, Harvard Medical School

"The most helpful business books start by defining a single fundamental obstacle that is overlooked or misunderstood. In *Influence and Impact,* that is: Most people don't understand their jobs, and without understanding your job becoming influential and making an impact are difficult at best. Fear not. As eminently qualified professionals and master coaches, Bill Berman and George Bradt have mapped a path to relevance. They invite you to take a deep dive into what your organization is really about. To excel in your career, you need to go deeper than org charts and truly divine your value toward achieving the group's mission. . .or understand when to walk away if there's too much misalignment. The authors present concise and relatable case studies of this quest. *Influence and Impact* reads like a boot camp for contributors, managers, and executives who are serious about advancing fulfilling careers."

Randall P White, Ph.D., Head of Leadership, eMBA, HEC, Paris and Founding Partner Executive Development Group LLC

Influence
and Impact

Influence and Impact

Discover and Excel at What Your
Organization Needs From You The Most

BILL BERMAN

GEORGE BRADT

WILEY

Published by John Wiley & Sons, Inc., Hoboken, New Jersey.
Published simultaneously in Canada.

For general information on our other products and services or for technical support,
please contact our Customer Care Department within the United States at (800) 762-
2974, outside the United States at (317) 572-3993 or fax (317) 572-4002.

Wiley publishes in a variety of print and electronic formats and by print-on-demand.
Some material included with standard print versions of this book may not be included
in e-books or in print-on-demand. If this book refers to media such as a CD or DVD
that is not included in the version you purchased, you may download this material
at http://booksupport.wiley.com. For more information about Wiley products, visit
www.wiley.com.

Library of Congress Cataloging-in-Publication Data is Available:

ISBN 978-1-119-78613-9 (Hardcover)
ISBN 978-1-119-78614-6 (ePDF)
ISBN 978-1-119-78615-3 (ePub)

Cover design: Paul McCarthy

SKY10026811_050521

Contents

Acknowledgments

We both owe a debt of gratitude to our colleagues of all types—coaches, human resources leaders, talent leaders, and business leaders. Each one has informed and improved our work. Naming them all would take a new book, but if you read this and think, "Do they mean me?" then the answer is "Yes!" You all have helped us learn and grow every time we worked together.

The hundreds of clients we have had over the past 15 years have taught us so much about human nature, and ourselves. You have given us the trust and respect to let us help you be who you are capable of being.

Our guest contributors have been phenomenal colleagues and allies. Each took time out of very busy lives to stop, read parts of the manuscript, and write their own thoughts to make the book stronger.

We owe endless thanks to our people at John Wiley and Sons. Our publisher, Richard Narramore, his associate, Victoria Anllo, and our editor, Deborah Schindlar, have consistently shown the trust and respect for us that is essential to writing partnerships. You made us much more intelligent and articulate than we really are. If you were make-up artists, we'd probably look like Paul Newman and Robert Redford.

Bill Berman:

I have had a number of mentors throughout my career who have supported, helped, advised, cajoled, and cheered me on as I have gone down this long and winding road called a career. Brendan Maher, Sidney Blatt, and Dennis Turk got me into psychology and into the real world. Jeremy Kisch taught me some useful lessons, and John Clarkin and Marv Reznikoff supported and fertilized my intellectual pursuits. Steve Hurt was the best back-office partner that a front-office entrepreneur could have. Joe Braga and John Raden also taught me a lot about being a leader of an organization. John Scott, Kathleen Lundquist, and the team at APTMetrics had the faith and trust in me to start me on my consulting psychology path. My colleagues and friends at PrimeGenesis helped me to understand the complexity of large public companies, and saw the benefit of having both business and psychological perspectives in our work together. My friends at the Society for Consulting Psychology, especially the board members and my study group partners, have taught me what it really means to have an impact on a larger organization. And, for the past 15 years, my co-author, colleague, and friend George has been a never-ending source of encouragement, challenge, and inspiration. I would not be at this point without all of your influences.

To the coaches who work with me at various clients, you have been wonderful partners and colleagues, and allowed me the room to write this book. Kristina Lalas, Lucienne Lunn, and Taylere Markewich have been my recent associates at Berman Leadership, and have made sure that everything I do is on time and of the highest quality, while keeping me focused on what is most important. I also want to express my appreciation to the psychotherapy patients I had the honor to work with before becoming a coach. You taught me about honesty, empathy, insight, forgiveness, and the value of self-awareness.

My wife, Ellen, has been a rock of consistency for me and for the family, providing love and caring, endlessly tolerant of my long work hours and my never-ending stream of projects. My children have been great in spite of what they call my slight case of ADHD: Daniel, Mandy, Jon, and Shane have supported and encouraged me, from reading drafts, to critiquing, to helping me keep my sense of humor and humility. My family of origin has had influence and impact for many decades—Jill, Richard, Kate, Brad and Ruth, and my late father Bill and mother Jean, who passed too soon. And of course, "The New Year's Eve Gang"—I would not be here without you.

George Bradt:

To Meg, who seems to greet every one of my new initiatives—from businesses to books to musical plays and everything in between—with a bemused look of "*Oh no. Not again,*" and ends up supporting everything I do in a way to which no one else on the planet could begin to come close, and has turned my focus from what I can do myself to how I can influence and impact others—abounding gratitude.

Influence and Impact

Introduction*

Enhance Your Influence and Impact by Focusing on the Mission-Critical Parts of Your Role and Adapting to the Culture of the Organization

Over the past 30 years, we have seen hundreds of people in our roles as coaches, consultants, line managers, entrepreneurs, and psychologists (Bill) and marketers (George). Many of these competent, capable leaders and professionals do most of their work very well, but still feel they are struggling to get the rewards, recognition, and growth that they are expecting.

Some have been in roles where they feel they are flying, but then things slow down. Others are in jobs where they are overwhelmed, overburdened, under-resourced, time-pressured, and feeling stressed, lonely, and exhausted. Still others feel a general sense of malaise, as though they are stuck in place, and do not look forward to going to work every day. Millions of workers, managers, and executives find themselves in this situation at some point in their career.

In most jobs, you find meaning and value by being able to influence others and have an impact on the organization and its mission. In all of the scenarios above, you likely feel you have lost your ability to influence the people around you. When your capacity to bring others along is diminished, or you are not

---

*We will use the 3rd person plural throughout the book, they/their/theirs, to avoid suggesting any of this applies to any gender status. All of the cases in the book are real, or a synthesis of multiple cases, but have been modified so that we can maintain the confidentiality of our clients.

contributing to your organization's overall success, your job satisfaction and engagement drop, your frustration increases, and your stress level rises.

Why does this happen so often? Sometimes, the reason truly is not under your control. In some cases, your manager is difficult or unsupportive, and is not likely to change. Sometimes, there are structural problems with the job, and there is no way to have influence or impact under the current framework. But this book is not for those situations. For a large majority of people, the struggle to have influence or impact and satisfaction in their work comes, not from external factors, but rather from something that they *are* able to manage and change.

What has become clear to us, through our work with people from CEOs to first-line managers, and even individual contributors, is that many people are unintentionally misunderstanding critical aspects of their job. When organizations send clients to us for executive coaching or onboarding, we look carefully at how they spend their time, how they think about their job, and how they do that job.

Many times, *we find that they are not focused on the essential elements of their job*. They may be doing someone else's job unintentionally. They may be trying to do their colleagues' jobs, either implicitly or by making a premature power grab to take on greater scope or responsibility. Sometimes, they are only doing one part of their job—the part they like, or the part that is most familiar.

Sometimes, when working with leaders, we find they are doing the right things, but in a way that is inconsistent with the style, attitudes, and mores of their organization. In some cases, they are decisive when they need to be collaborative. They are direct and blunt when they need to be tactful and patient.

One client, Ian, worked in a formal banking setting. Everyone wore Zegna suits or St. James knits, but he persisted in wearing casual clothes. This leader was doing the right work, but his style and approach undermined his ability to influence other bankers. He was fortunate to have a senior manager watching out for him. As he gave him a promotion to lead a business unit, he told him, "You are to throw out all your shirts and sweaters, and I'm taking you shopping. You have to look the part I know you can play."

Some people do this because they believe that their approach has worked in the past, or was appropriate for the last organization they were in. They may feel that their style is core to their identity, and to change it would be to change who they are. Or they may not have thought about their approach at all, doing what comes naturally rather than making a conscious and deliberate effort to act in a way that works within the current context.

To repeat the most important point of this introduction, and this book, people lose their ability to influence others and impact the organization because they are not focused on the most essential, mission-critical business and cultural priorities. They usually do not even know what those are! Often, organizations and managers are not as explicit as they should be about the focus of their employees' work, the culture of the organization, or their own needs and expectations.

The really great news is that despite these common challenges, you can enhance your influence and impact by focusing on the mission-critical parts of your role (the business) without anyone explicitly telling you what they are. You can be more effective by learning about and adapting to the behaviors, relationships and mores of the organization (the culture)—or you may realize, after reading the first parts of this book, that it's just not a fit and you would flourish more in a different organization.

What is influence? What is impact? How are they different? Influence is the indirect or intangible effect you have on others, based on what you do, how you do it, how you communicate it, and who you are. Impact is the direct and observable effect you have on the entities you deal with—your manager, your team, your organization. We are particularly focused on helping you improve the effect you have on others—your influence—in ways that result in a significant or major effect on your manager, your team, and your organization—your impact.

This is the key to professional success in organizations: Doing the job that is needed, in the way that is needed, consistently and effectively. Managers, leaders, and executives can do this by understanding the essential, but often unwritten or implicit, parts of their job, and the unwritten or implicit aspects of the organizational culture. Developing an enhanced focus, delivered in a manner that is aligned with what their job is invariably results in more influence with other people, and a larger impact on the organization and its mission.

Why You Need This Book

People work for different reasons. For some, it is simply to have enough money to live their life the way they want. For others, it is a passion, something they do to feel fulfilled. But whatever the reason, having influence on others, and an impact on the organization you work for, is going to make you feel good about what you are doing. One of the major sources of job satisfaction is feeling that you make a difference, that you have an effect on the people you work with and the organization you work for. Whether you are looking to climb the corporate ladder, or find gratification in your current job, having influence and impact on others will boost your happiness and gratitude.

We provide a set of steps that will help you understand yourself and your role, and use that understanding to influence your organization: How to know what is needed, deliver that consistently, communicate about all of this effectively. The method is straightforward and draws on our decades of experience as coaches, consultants to executives, and executives ourselves.

Part I explains what you are doing that interferes with your influence and impact, why that is hurting your job satisfaction, and how to resolve it. We help you identify what distracts you, and why. Once you understand the disconnect between what you are doing and what the organization needs, you can commit to making the changes that will allow you to succeed, flourish and be recognized for doing important work—maybe even get a promotion!

This is a significant mindset shift, as well as a behavior change. To be successful, you must acknowledge that your job may not be what you were told it was. It may not be what you thought it would be, or what you want it to be. At the same time, you have to figure out what matters to you about your job. This knowledge will help you focus on what is really critical to success in your job. In addition, you have to learn how to interact, communicate, and work with others in ways that work in your current context.

Part II is designed to help you sort out what your boss, your team, and your organization *really* need from you, both from a business and a cultural perspective. This is not a solo exercise. You will need to enlist a range of stakeholders, including your manager, your colleagues, and your team, to help you solve this. The methods we recommend are derived from common parts of our executive coaching work, but are focused as much on the broader context than they are on the individual.

We recognize that *not all cultures should be adapted to*. The history of bias, discrimination, and exclusion in work settings is inescapable. Sometimes the term "cultural fit" can be a cover for conscious or unconscious exclusion practices. This is a special case and requires a thoughtful approach to what's really going on, how you adapt, and how you change things. Dr. Greg Pennington has written the chapter on how to think about and deal with bias and discrimination in the workplace with a calibration, information, demonstration, negotiation, and transformation framework.

When you study your role more deeply, you may realize the problem is easy to fix; or, that your manager is impossible, the job is impossible, or the organization is wrong (at least for you). Once you discover what the underlying expectations are for you (and they are probably unspoken), you then have to ask yourself a very difficult question—do I still want my job? Is this what will make me happy? For some, this will be obvious; for others, this may come as a shock. A number of you will discover, "Wow! That's why I'm struggling. I'm in the wrong job!"

Our experience is that most clients, when they discover how they can have much more impact and influence in their jobs, get really energized. They stop doing stuff they've done for years, try out new skills, make some mistakes, but after a few months realize they are much happier with the new perspective they have on their job.

Part III describes the path you take if you want the job you are in. This section takes you through the nuts and bolts of creating a Personal Strategic Plan to implement critical changes to your priorities, tone, and behavior that you discovered to be misaligned in Part II. This includes not only what you need to do differently, but how to work on it, practice it, and make it a part of how you operate.

Part IV is the path you take if you realize that the real job your organization wants you to do is not what you want or can do. For some people, they really like the organization they work for, but the specific job is a bad fit, or they just can't find a way to work happily with their manager. For others, this process helps them to realize that both the job they are doing and the context in which they work are not acceptable to them. Part IV has guidelines and recommendations for how to work your way out, if you realize you would be happier and more engaged with your work somewhere else.

This book is primarily for you to help yourself; but, if you're a manager, it's also your job to help your people go through this same process, to maximize their influence and impact in the organization. From first-line supervisors to CEOs and Board Chairs, helping direct reports focus on the essential priorities and methods is crucial. We wrote **Part V** as a primer for managers who want guidance on how to coach others to great influence and impact.

Most people will benefit from Parts I and II. These two sections lay the groundwork for rest of the book. At the end of Part II you are faced with a decision: Are you in the right job, the wrong job at the right company, or the wrong job at the wrong company? Based on your answer from Part II, you can then jump to Part III, if you know you want to make the changes you need to make. If you realize you do not want the job as it really is, or cannot operate the way the organization wants you to, some of Part III and Part IV will be the most helpful. For managers and executives, you may choose to jump all the way to Part V first, which is designed to help you guide your people toward what you and your organization need from them the most.

All of the worksheets and additional materials can be downloaded from **www.bermanleadership.com/InfluenceAndImpact**

PART I

The Disconnect: What Your Organization Wants You to Know (But Hasn't Told You!)

CHAPTER 1

Get What You Want by Doing What Your Organization Needs

The One Change You Need to Make

"Sometimes doing your best is not good enough. Sometimes you must do what is required."

—Winston S. Churchill

You know the feeling when you are on a roll at work. You get good reviews, and you are recognized and rewarded by your manager. You look forward to going to work, and feel challenged, stimulated, and "on your front foot." You are doing things you like and doing them well. You are proud of your work.

What makes this so special? It's a great feeling when people at work are interested in you, and appreciate what you do. That is, in a nutshell, influence. Influence means that other people take the time to listen to you, consider what you have to say, and want to work with you. Having impact is all about having a substantive effect on the organization, by leading without formal authority. Your colleagues know you are adding value to the organization, and to them. Influence and impact are the keys to job engagement and job satisfaction. Whether you are a technician using specialized skills or a business leader driving strategy and inspiring and enabling the organization, having influence and impact turns an average job into a personal growth experience.

Most of us have found ourselves in the converse situation at some point. Work is going "OK," but you find yourself in your job for longer than you planned. You feel like others are not listening to your ideas or paying attention to your input. Maybe you worked your tail off to help your boss turn things around, only to get a mediocre review and bonus. Or, you finally got the promotion you were looking for, only to see yourself struggling to achieve expectations, and hearing feedback that, "Things are going a little slower than we expected." You feel that you have lost your edge.

When it's missing, you know it. Human beings are fundamentally social beings. We love interpersonal feedback and connections that establish and reinforce who we are.[i] We spend as much time working as we do on anything else in our lives. Most of us want to find value and purpose in what we do. We need to feel we have agency, and we need to feel connected to others.[ii]

Writers and theorists have different labels for these needs, but they always include notions about independence, connectedness, security, recognition, impact, and having a clear sense of self. When you aren't getting this from your manager or your organization, to the degree you want or need them, you feel the gap and it creates disappointment. And, to paraphrase Yoda from Star Wars, disappointment leads to frustration, frustration leads to anger, anger leads eventually to getting another job. Bill learned a lesson at an early age in how to find value and meaning in doing what your company needs.

At age 15, I took a job as a sales associate in a camera store in downtown Washington, D.C. The store was right on Pennsylvania Avenue, between the White House and the Capital. My objective that summer was to earn enough money to use the discount the owner offered to buy a used Nikon F-1. My dream was to become a professional photographer, and the F-1 was the premier 35mm professional camera. What I did not realize was that very few people who came to the store wanted to talk about fancy cameras or lenses. Most of the people were tourists, walking from one monument to another, and came in either because they needed film, or they could not figure out how to work some basic part of their camera.

After about the 125th person came in and asked me how to rewind the film, or which button to push for zoom, my frustration began to boil over: "If you bothered to read the manual, you would know that the zoom button is right here," I said, clearly disgusted. The owner saw this and took me aside. "Bill, you came here to sell cameras, but that is not why you are here. You are here to sell film and film developing, because that is what keeps the store running. I need you to talk nice to the customers, answer their questions, no matter how simple, and provide good customer support. If you do that, more people will buy film or get their pictures developed here. That's how we make money. If you treat them poorly, they will go somewhere else. Your job is to get them to come back for those purchases. So, go, be nice, and solve their very simple problems for them."

At first, I was demoralized. I was going to spend the sweltering D.C. summer being bored. Ironically, I was already frustrated and disappointed because, at age 15, I was not aware of the underlying value of my job. My real job was to make customers feel taken care of. After this lecture from my boss, people's simplistic questions stopped being annoying, because I understood what my boss and the customers needed from me the most, and adapted to that.

What Gets in the Way?

So, what is the disconnect between you and what your organization needs from you most? What causes you to feel stuck, or stalled, that you aren't having the impact you want? How can you bring more value to your company and meaning for yourself? In many situations, you are making one or two simple but consequential mistakes: You are not focused on the mission-critical parts of your responsibilities, or you are not doing them in the way that the organization can understand and embrace.

"Wait, what?" you think. "I have objectives. I review these with my manager. How could I be doing the wrong things?" You may be doing the right things at one level, but when you dig a little deeper, you may find you are off the mark—though your boss might also be unaware, because they are focused on doing what they have always done rather than adapting to the current reality of what the organization needs. Or, you may be communicating or interacting in the way that the organizational culture cannot understand or appreciate.[iii]

What we have found, again and again, is that people tend to underperform because they do what is comfortable, what is familiar, or what they desire, rather than what is most important to the organization. The majority of people we have coached believed they were doing the right things, but they did not understand the organization's top priorities. A smaller proportion knew that they weren't doing the right work but were unable to change their mindset so that they could do the work right.

Regardless of whether their choices were conscious or unconscious, they all found themselves stalled, frustrated, and under-recognized and under-appreciated by their manager or their company. Is any of this true for you?

Doing What Is Easier

One of the most common causes of losing influence and impact is when you find yourself doing your direct reports' jobs instead of your own. You feel pressured and stressed and find it more comfortable to do work yourself than to give it to someone who works for you. There are a number of reasons, all of them valid to some degree:

"It's faster for me to do it."

"I don't want to overburden my people. I'll take it on."

"They aren't skilled, and I don't have the time to teach or coach them."

"It has to be done just right, and I don't have people who can do it as well as I can."

Each one of these feels right and may be true in the short run. But at some point, your people start to feel that they aren't growing, and feel their value is eroding just as yours is.

Tommy was known for having a blend of technological, operational, and business expertise that helped him rise to become the leader of a 1500-person business unit spanning four continents. He knew the economics of his business and was able convert his skills into practical technology and process solutions. But like many people, his strengths were also his weaknesses. Because Tommy understood the business in such depth, he often knew the answers well before his team did. As a result, he would identify the solution, inform others, and tell them to execute. He spent a lot of time evaluating their work, making adjustments, and providing direction. Unsurprisingly, his team resented what felt to them like micromanaging. Tommy felt overworked and underappreciated. His team felt undervalued, under-challenged, and demoralized.

His boss asked one of us (Bill) to work with Tommy—to help him focus on what she needed most from Tommy: Enterprise strategy, reorganization, offshoring, and cross-business collaboration.

As we worked together, Tommy acknowledged that his impatience to get to a solution often made him annoyed at his team members, and he expressed frustration when he found himself sitting in a meeting, knowing the answer, and not hearing anyone tell him the solution.

I asked, "Why do you need to sit in those meetings? What would happen if you asked them to come up with solutions and present them to you?"

Tommy quickly began to realize that he was avoiding the more complex and long-term aspects of his work where he had less confidence.

His core job was to build collaborative relationships with senior leaders of lines of business, manage groups whose objectives and rewards were in conflict with his, and deal with complex problems that had no obvious solution.

> *Tommy stepped back and let his team sort out the operational problems. He discovered that, without his involvement, they often came up with reasonable solutions. And when they did not initially find a reasonable answer, he started redirecting them and letting them go back to work the problem more.*
>
> *Tommy's boss eventually noticed that he had freed up time, and told him, "I've been waiting for you to figure this out." As Tommy confronted his self-doubts, he was able to focus more on the high-level relationships and the complex challenges that really deserved his attention.*

Sometimes it is faster to do it yourself. Or, you may just fall back on what you find to be rewarding or gratifying. Think of this like "mowing the lawn," or "doing the dishes," because the tasks are simple, well-defined, and have a beginning and an end. They rarely require the level of skill the individual brings to the table, but it is much easier (to continue the analogy) to wash the dishes than to figure out how to redesign the kitchen to include a dishwasher.

Tip for Leaders

Just because you are better at some things than your people are doesn't mean you should do them. Your technical expertise is important. But that is not what you are paid for, and when you dive into a problem that calls for your technical expertise you lose hours of the most precious commodity of all—time. And your people learn nothing. Because you did the work yourself, your organization is no better equipped to do the work next time. You unintentionally teach your people to do sloppy jobs, since they know you will overrule or fix their work. They stop bringing their A game.

Doing the Job You Wish You Had

One of the quickest paths to losing influence and impact comes from trying to do jobs that belong to your colleagues. Many clients have told us, "My colleagues aren't getting their work done! And when they do, it's inadequate. That prevents me and my team from being successful. They should let me take that on." These individuals rarely see themselves as self-interested. They are trying to help their manager, or the organization, succeed more quickly or operate more efficiently. They are trying to have more impact.

But the results are bad. Colleagues come to believe that you see yourself as smarter, more experienced, or more capable than them. They see you as self-interested or self-promoting. This creates a negative spiral in which your influence and impact drops precipitously. Peers stop cooperating. This causes you to push harder since less work is getting done, which increases their lack of collaboration. One person Bill observed while working with a start-up fell into this trap.

> *Rohit was hired to manage consumer marketing for a start-up clothing company, based on several years' experience in a large company, where he developed a fledgling direct-to-consumer segment for the company. When he arrived, he was given responsibility for print and e-business development, while social media, institutional sales, and private label deals were left to others.*
>
> *Almost immediately, Rohit started lobbying to take over other marketing functions. First, he sought responsibility for social media, arguing that the two had sufficient overlap that they needed to be managed together. At the same time, he pushed to take over institutional sales. He argued that the experience from his previous company made him more qualified than anyone else in the organization.*
>
> *Unfortunately, Rohit had not yet demonstrated any growth in the direct-to-consumer segment. His peers found his efforts to take control arrogant and irritating. The CEO insisted that he demonstrate success in his own sphere before taking on any other roles. In spite of this, he kept lobbying to take on more responsibility, which frustrated everyone. The CEO rapidly lost confidence in him because of his lack of success in his primary role, and became increasingly intolerant of his attitude.*

Instead of taking on colleagues' jobs, some individuals try to take on their own manager's job. We observe this less often, probably because the manager usually moves to stop the behavior quickly. For some people, however, they do not seem to understand the difference between their job and their manager's job, and eventually end up in a power struggle to prove they are equals.

A corollary of this is the person who believes they do not have to discuss their activities or decisions with their manager and should be given total autonomy to make decisions and take action within their remit, without input or oversight. The consistent message we have heard from these individuals is, "I know how to do my job. Why does my manager need to get involved in 'the details?'"

Doing What Is Familiar

Some people we have worked with struggled because they were uncomfortable with the responsibilities of their new job. Often, when someone is promoted, they do not immediately understand what the expectations are. Moreover, the new job frequently requires knowledge and skills that weren't required before, which makes them feel insecure. One recently promoted manager said, anxiously, "They handed me a report and told me to come to a meeting to discuss it. I don't have any idea what the report means!"

As first-time managers, you may not feel comfortable directing others, or giving feedback. As senior leaders, you may find you are managing people who know much more about the subject matter than you do. Handling these transitions requires three things: Comfort with uncertainty; familiarity with your generalizable skills; and deliberate and effortful thinking.

Because of discomfort with not knowing all the answers, many people risk falling back on what Nobel Prize winner Daniel Kahneman describes as intuitive thinking.[iv] You revert to established knowledge from the last job you had. Kahneman summed up the argument in his *2002 Nobel Prize Lecture*. In it, he described intuition as "thoughts and preferences that come to mind quickly and without much reflection," as opposed to a more controlled, structured way of thinking things through.

If you are using your intuitive or "System 1" thinking to solve the problems of a new job, you are likely managing at too low a level, underutilizing your team, or responding with short-term moves rather than proactive efforts to drive the business forward.

Kristy was a skilled product development leader who understood the systems and processes needed to bring products to market. Her manager, Aaron, valued her work and knew he could count on her to deliver on their quarterly objectives. At the same time, Aaron knew that customer needs were rapidly evolving and saw Kristy focusing on the short-term rather than the mid- to long-term. As a result, Aaron had concerns that Kristy would not be able to help the firm take advantage of new technologies to accelerate change and anticipate new trends.

Kristy and her team were working on 12 product development initiatives, but she made the vast majority of decisions herself. She was frustrated that her people were not stepping up to take responsibility. I (Bill) asked her what would happen if she had the right people to lead these initiatives, and she half-joked, "I'm not sure I know what my job would be."

In reality, Kristy's job would become what Aaron was looking for: forward-thinking, change-focused, and strategic. As she grew to understand that, she reworked ten of the 12 initiatives into four major strategies, and stopped two of the initiatives that did not fit the framework. Team members each led one strategy, and they clearly defined the decision rights and escalation criteria.

Kristy's team meetings shifted from weekly tactical decision-making to bi-weekly oversight, challenge and course-correction, while bi-monthly meetings became more future-focused and talent-focused. After a few weeks, Kristy found that she had free time, and began working on an innovation white paper that became a potential road-map for a new product framework for the company.

Doing What You Expected

Doing exactly the job in your job description, rather than the job the company or your manager needs you to do, does not help you influence anyone. The need for flexibility is common in start-ups, where most job descriptions say, at the bottom, ". . .and any other responsibilities as they are identified by your manager." Successful people in start-ups and fast-growth companies often need to learn new skills, shift between two different sets of responsibilities, or multi-task. In more stable, large companies, a "can-do" spirit is invaluable, but people often learn to only do what their job description says. Unfortunately, this does not build your reputation as a problem solver or "go-to" person.

Sarah took a job at a cloud-based technology company as a software trainer. Her job was to learn how the software works and put together and deliver training programs to the end users. She enjoyed getting in front of a group, using technology, and showing them how to use the system. She found it gratifying to see people learn the skills she had to teach.

When her company was bought by a larger software company, a number of people left, and her new manager asked her to take responsibility for implementing the software as well as do the training. She politely but firmly refused, stating, "I'm a trainer. I don't want to do implementation. It's boring." Her manager explained that the implementation team was stretched thin, and in order for her to have enough training to do, she would need to help with the implementation as well. Despite this, she again refused.

You can imagine what happened. In three months, as soon as the amount of training work decreased, she was the first to be let go.

Doing It "Your Own Way"

Influence comes when you can work and communicate with colleagues in ways that say, "We are on the same team." Your organization has a set of cultural norms that determine how people share information, make decisions, and work with each other. These mores are rarely explicit, but they are widely shared and reflect the organization's needs, motivations, and beliefs.

In particular, people often think about their relationship with their manager differently from how the manager defines it. Your manager, and your manager's manager, have sets of implicit norms that are usually subsets of the organization's rules. For example, if your manager is insecure, they may rely on you to support them rather than supporting you. If the functional head is a "bias to action" leader, they may think everyone should operate the same way.

Many times, the company's explicit values are different from the behaviors and attitudes they reinforce in reality. Learning the organizational and team culture will increase your cultural agility, which has value in any new setting. Listening and communicating effectively is essential to increasing your influence and impact. Adapting to the culture-as-is is critical to getting the types of rewards and reinforcements you are looking for.

Whom We Tend to Blame—And Why It Doesn't Work

It is human nature to want to blame other people for the problems in which we find ourselves.[v] Our sense of self tells us we are right, and that problems arise because others have misunderstood our intent, or because they are unfair or have ulterior motives. Some people blame themselves, but the majority maintain personal equilibrium by externalizing problems, even though that may not lead to the best solution.

Linda had been brought in by the president of a small company, Akito, as his head of HR. In reality, he really wanted Linda to handle many tactical and operational issues that he, as CEO, did not want to deal with. She sat in on meetings and frequently provided direction to other team leaders, even though she had no involvement in their work. If anyone challenged her, she pushed back by drawing on the CEO's authority. "Akito made it clear to me that he expects this from you."

The team was clearly unhappy with her ambiguous role, and developed a noticeable passivity toward her directives. I (Bill) was brought in by Akito to help Linda be more effective, but when I tried to help her find ways to give direction, through influence or from her own authority, she rejected the idea that she should do anything different. "They just resent my relationship with Akito. If they don't improve, we may have to find other people who will listen."

Focusing on Your Manager

Managers make or break a job experience.[vi] The problems with managers are legion—from micromanagers to laissez-faire, from domineering to passive, and from abusive to neglectful. Some managers are poor managers. Some were promoted because they were a strong front-line worker, or they have seniority. Others are given unrealistic responsibilities and are browbeaten themselves. More have the right technical skills but have no training or experience in managing. Management is, after all, a learned skill rather than an innate talent.

At least as often, there is a mismatch in style or misalignment of objectives between manager and employee. When the two expect different things, or have different workstyles, problems are likely to follow. A hands-off manager may be exactly what one person, who is self-confident, risk-taking and focused, needs to be successful. That same manager may be exactly the wrong one for a person who needs clear, specific direction, tries to avoid missteps, and works best with detailed plans and timelines.

When you and your manager are misaligned, tensions grow. It invariably leads to anger and disappointment for both. For example, an employee thinks their job is to collaborate with their manager to develop ideas and brainstorm in a meeting, while the manager is expecting a well-considered proposal with pros and cons and a recommendation. Unless the team member accepts the manager's view of the job, they are frustrated by the manager's refusal to help them, and the manager views the employee as underperforming.

We try to get our managers to give us what we think we need, or what has worked for us in the past. But as a supervisor once advised, "Bill, you'll be much happier if you figure out what your supervisor is good at and learn that. Trying to get your supervisor to give you what you think you need to learn is much more frustrating."

Focusing on Your Team

People often attribute problems at work to the people who work for them. Just as employees tend to blame their managers for many problems, managers tend to think that failures or misses are due to "weak players" and look for ways to replace them. Both authors have known managers who have an endless cycle of replacing team members, all at once or one at a time, never stopping to think that the problem may be themselves instead of their team.

Replacing team members may be necessary, particularly when a new leader comes into a role and has a different vision, strategy, or mandate than the prior one. At some point it is the job of a leader to make the most of the people they have rather than continuously blaming the individuals for what is actually their own responsibility. The manager's manager and others start to notice this pattern of blaming the team members, and the problem with the team becomes a problem with the manager. Before long, the organization is looking for a new leader, rather than new players.

Focusing on Your Company

Just as there are managers whom no one can work for, and teams that need to be replaced, there are companies whose vision, culture, and values are either objectively wrong, or wrong for you. When you find yourself working for a company that is focused on self-enrichment, and your values lead you to provide for others, you may need to consider moving on. However, attributing difficulties in your job performance to the company may mask the difficulties you have in adapting to the environment you are in. You may be externalizing responsibility for your own difficulty accepting that we all have to adapt to our environment to survive. Keep in mind that, unless you are in a position of significant authority, you are not likely to substantively change the company you work for.

Why Externalizing Rarely Works

Attributing responsibility to others severely limits your options. If you see the difficulties as lying outside of what you are doing and how you are doing it, you can only do two things: Try to get the "other" to change or find a better "other." The former is difficult, because the others feel blamed, which makes them angry, hurt, and defensive. Moreover, the behaviors you find problematic likely have been working for them. The latter is time-consuming, and you have no guarantee that a new job is going to give you a better experience than your current one.

By contrast, assuming responsibility for finding a solution to feeling like you aren't succeeding gives you a wide range of options to develop and demonstrate your value. Even if you do decide that the current situation needs to be changed, we recommend spending some time making sure you are doing what is really needed to succeed before jumping ship.

Getting Unstuck

In summary, many of our efforts to contribute to the organization paradoxically cause us to lose influence and impact. We try to do more, or do what we know best, or what feels safe, unconsciously leading us to detract from our value and weaken our impact. The actions we take are a response to our attitudes, emotions, and underlying beliefs about ourselves, others, and our organizational context. The good news is that you have the ability to turn the tables and increase your agency and effectiveness. What you prioritize, where you and your team focus attention, and how you act, respond, and communicate can be changed to make it clear you are aligned to your manager, your function and the organization.

To be clear, there are times when the feeling of being stuck has nothing to do with you. You may be in a bad situation or there is a difference in values or style that cannot be overcome. Until you find that out, however, you have many more degrees of freedom when you focus on yourself. Start by framing the problem as something you can control, and change may be more actionable than trying to change others or looking for a new job. Our next chapter will make it clear how you can enhance your value to the organization, and help you expand your influence and impact on others.

Key Takeaways

Get what you want by doing what your organization needs. The one change you need to make is to shift your attention from the temptations of doing what is comfortable, what is familiar, or what you wish, to doing what is most important to the organization.

End Notes

[i] Cooley, C. H. (1992). *Human nature and the social order.* Transaction Publishers.; Mead, G. H. (1962). *Mind, self, and society.* Chicago: University of Chicago.

[ii] Maslow, A. H. (1943). "A theory of human motivation." *Psychological Review,* 50: 396.; Hogan, K. (2011). *The science of influence: How to get anyone to say yes in 8 minutes or less.* Hoboken, NJ: Wiley.; Rock, D. (2008). "SCARF: A brain-based model for collaborating with and influencing others." *NeuroLeadership Journal,* 1: 44–52.

[iii] Mehrabian, A. (1981). *Silent messages: Implicit communication of emotions and attitudes.* Belmont, CA: Wadsworth.

[iv] Bradt, G. (2019, October). As an executive onboarding into a new role, engage intellectually, emotionally and practically—in that order. Forbes. Retrieved February 7, 2021 from https://www.forbes.com/sites/georgebradt/2019/10/22/as-an-executive-onboarding-into-a-new-role-engage-intellectually-emotionally-and-practically--in-that-order/?sh=58d89f9d5be6; Kahneman, D. (2011). *Thinking, fast and slow.* New York: Farrar, Straus and Giroux.

[v] Forester, J., & McKibbon, G. (2020). Beyond blame: Leadership, collaboration and compassion in the time of COVID-19. *Socio-Ecological Practice Research,* 2(3): 205–216.

[vi] Reina, C. S., Rogers, K. M., Peterson, S. J., Byron, K., & Hom, P. W. (2018). Quitting the boss? The role of manager influence tactics and employee emotional engagement in voluntary turnover. *Journal of Leadership & Organizational Studies,* 25(1): 5–18.

CHAPTER 2

You Have More Power than You Realize

"Seek out that particular mental attribute which makes you feel most deeply and vitally alive, along with which comes the inner voice which says, 'This is the real me,' and when you have found that attitude, follow it."

—William James, *The Principles of Psychology*

The Solution, Step 1. Accept the Context

The first step to increasing your influence and impact is developing a clear understanding and acceptance of your situation *as it is currently*. Most people erroneously believe that the role they need to do is what is in their job description. In addition, we usually assume that what we expect from our manager and our company is consistent with what the manager and the company accept as their responsibility. This is known as the psychological contract[i] with your organization. Unlike written contracts, however, the psychological contract is implied, not explicit and ever-evolving. Realizing that what you thought your job was may not be what your organization actually needs from you can be extremely upsetting.

> Lionel was furious. "We were supposed to be equal partners!" he explained, telling me (Bill) how he had brought the idea to his business partner, Edgar, and had convinced him that the gene-splicing approach he proposed was really breakthrough. They were both going to contribute, and would co-lead the organization. "Now, it's as though this was his idea all along, and I'm excluded from meetings I should be in!"
>
> After a few minutes, Lionel said snidely, "I know, I can't change anyone but myself, right? Isn't that what you people always say?"
>
> We shifted focus to how Lionel might be contributing to Edgar treating him this way. We hypothesized that what Edgar wanted and needed was someone who handled all research and development, and kept the scientists engaged, which he did not know how to do. Edgar wanted control of anything affecting customers and investors, which he felt were his natural strengths.
>
> We concluded that Lionel's working title should be Head of Research and Development, regardless of what his explicit job title was. Lionel focused his time and energy on the scientific mission, where he consistently excelled. As a result, Edgar became less involved, less critical, and more open to Lionel's input and ideas, even though he still did not embrace Lionel as an equal.

Accept Your Emotions

We all have hopes, expectations and needs. They are the fundamental elements of happiness. When those needs are met, we feel gratified. When others expect something different, we become frustrated. If our organization or manager expect different things from what we need, the normal human response is to feel disrespected or controlled. This can produce a spiral of negative emotions and self-protective thoughts. We rationalize and justify our position and have extended internal dialogues (and sometimes external monologues with family, friends or colleagues) that "prove" that the problem lies with others.

Accepting your emotions without acting on them is the key to resolving them. Often our "emotional" behaviors—hostility, withdrawal, complaining— are designed to make the feeling go away. Try to accept and understand your feelings. At the same time, develop the self-awareness and self-acceptance to embrace them as a source of data while you sort out what *about you* needs to change.

Accept That You Are Not in Control of the Job

Control, autonomy, and the need for respect are major motivators for people. The higher you move in an organization, the more likely you are to find people who value independence and self-determination. These drivers are linked to the ambition that leads people to want to succeed in organizations.

Nevertheless, it is essential to accept that you are not in control of the job you have—especially in a larger, hierarchical organization with its own objectives. In companies like that, at least five people had input into your job description, including the hiring manager, human resources, at least one or two people senior to the hiring manager, as well as finance. And they had never met you.

Accept That No One Is Perfect and That Everyone Needs to Adapt to Be Effective

Take a deep breath and accept that you have flaws just like everyone else. There are usually one or two things anyone could improve, as your best friends will tell you if they care enough. Your manager may think that you are the right person for the role, but they are unlikely to think you are ideal.

No one can force you to change your values, attitudes, expectations and behaviors. There is extensive social science research, however, that indicates that your ability to adjust to the context you live or work in is directly related to the likelihood of your success.[ii]

> *Hélène had been raised in China before attending graduate school in the Boston area. When she took a job in strategy after graduation, she struggled to tell her manager that she thought his ideas for an acquisition were unrealistic. She had been socialized to avoid disagreement with superiors. As a result, she worked for several months on a due diligence she never expected to be successful. When her manager found out, he recommended she get a coach. Our work focused on her need to adapt to her current environment, where disagreement and challenge with her manager was expected. She quickly began to embrace the culture, and disagreed with her boss when he opposed a recommended acquisition. She argued successfully, and the acquisition was a win for both of them.*

The Solution, Step 2. Rediscover Your Value*

Self-awareness is essential to improving your ability to influence and impact others. No one works well in all contexts, and everyone has characteristics that work in some environments better than others. Knowing yourself includes knowing your strengths and style, your motivations, values and preferences. In addition, awareness of your long-term objectives increases the likelihood that you will achieve them. As every automobile driving instructor will tell you, keep your eyes focused on where you want the car to go, and the car will go there; if you look at the obstacle in the road, the car is likely to go toward that.

There are formal and informal ways of understanding yourself. Honest self-reflection may be the only one available to you right now. Getting feedback from others, or from objective sources, however, can be extremely helpful. Knowing how others see you is an essential part of knowing yourself, because it is important for you to know how others interpret your actions. Since they do not necessarily know your intentions, how you come across to others can be very different than how you think of yourself.[iii] One of the most common disconnects we find in our work is when a client's behavior is interpreted by others very differently than it was intended.

> Sandy was a dynamic, strategic leader who motivated her people through a combination of enthusiasm and clear purpose. She was always exploring options, looking for new product lines and pushing innovation. To her, this was stimulating and exciting work. She was surprised when she was told that some of her people were demoralized and frustrated. She asked for a series of 360° interviews to understand the problem. What she heard back was that she was constantly shifting gears, making people work long hours on a new project only to have it sidelined repeatedly. Her intention—to explore new opportunities, which she found endlessly exciting—was experienced to be inconsistent, reactive, and destabilizing. She decided to create a "skunkworks" function, and carefully picked people who viewed the innovation efforts the way she did—challenging and fun.

---

*NOTE: there are scientifically reliable and valid tools to formally assess almost everything we discuss in this chapter, from individual characteristics to organizational culture. All of these methods, to our knowledge, require multiple raters to provide useful information. As a result, what we provide here are simplified methods for an individual to garner, as unobtrusively as possible, what the essential characteristics are for their role. Our assessments may not be comprehensive, and you may want to address different issues, or define them differently. Feel free—remember, the objective is to gather data that will help you upgrade YOUR job, not fill in our templates.

Creating Your Authentic Leadership

Guest Contributor: Carol Kauffman, Ph.D., ABPP

What is the foundation for being able to influence others?

The foundation of influence is knowing the truth about yourself first, then others. You need to be self-aware, centered, able to be curious and compassionate to the experience of the person you are trying to influence.

How do you know the truth about yourself? There are many pathways. The one I'll share is very similar to "You've got this!" To upgrade your job, upgrade yourself.

For about six years I had the privilege of working with Bill George and Scott Snook from Harvard Business School and the Authentic Leadership Institute and first the top 20, then the top 300 leaders at Unilever, then AstraZeneca and other organizations. This journey culminated in *The Discover Your True North Fieldbook: A Personal Guide to Finding Your Authentic Leadership* by Nick Craig with Bill and Scott. This guide is an excellent follow-up once you've introduced yourself to the powerful concepts laid out here by George and Bill.

The program followed a series of steps. First is a powerful introduction. Imagine telling someone who you are without reference to anything on your resume. Then sharing what experiences have made you who you are today. These can be from your childhood, early life.

To know who you really are, you also need to look at what Warren Bennis calls "Crucibles." These are experiences so challenging and "hot" that they transformed who you are. When thinking about your most difficult experiences ask, How has surviving these helped me become a better leader and person? You may not have stopped to think this through before. Doing so in tandem with the exercises in this chapter will help you on that journey.

The next steps are knowing your intrinsic and extrinsic motivations. What gives you energy? Is it learning, teamwork, achievement? Then, How can you align your job to what energizes you? There are many roads to Rome, figure out which pathway to your goal works best for you.

What you love doing is usually connected to your strengths. A free strengths test is available at **VIACharacter.org**. When you've completed that, layer your strengths onto the four areas described in this chapter. There are many ways to be technically brilliant or build business savvy. So, know your strengths. Then, when you face a gap between where you are and where you need to go, see if you can create a bridge to the other side of the challenge by using one of your strengths in a new way.

If you want to influence others you need to know your values. When you do, you are more able to understand the values of others. Putting your own values and the other person's values together, along with understanding your own story, how you've survived, your motivations and strengths can show you the way forward to your own optimal performance and well-being. Then you can understand these in others and become an authentic and inspirational leader.

Examine Your Style

Some people spend weeks or months going into deep self-reflection and self-exploration. Others may be tempted to ignore this part of the data collection completely, thinking "I am who I am, and I am not going to change." We recommend a middle ground, where you spend enough time on this to have a reasonable grasp of how you react under stress, and what may cause you problems when you aren't at your best. Do you withdraw and protect yourself? Do you take the approach of "Damn the torpedoes, full speed ahead!?" Do you get analysis paralysis or avoid making a choice? How you act, and what you prefer, are only a small part of this data collection. As we said above, this process can be iterative, and you can come back to self-awareness in the future.

There are a variety of ways to know both your people-focused and work-focused personal style (personality). One way to know yourself is to take a personality assessment. Personality tests are typically reliable, validated self-report measures of key personality traits based on decades of psychological research on personality. These assessments tend to classify you into specific categories, (for example, the Myers–Briggs[iv] or the DISC[v]) or dimensions of personality (such as the Hogan® Series[vi] or the 16PF[vii]). The website **PsychCentral.com** (**https://psychcentral.com/personality-test/start.php**) provides what is called a "Big Five" assessment. If you want in particular to take the Myers–Briggs test, the publishers offer an online version (**https://www.mbtionline. com/en-US/Products/For-you**).

Strengths, Opportunities for Growth, Values, and Preferences

Start by collecting some basic data about yourself. What are the most important things you should know about yourself? There are four domains for you to focus on.

Strengths

Strengths are the things you do particularly well, based on past training, jobs, feedback, and experience. They are a combination of your talents, your knowledge, and your skills. Talents are typically thought of as naturally occurring capabilities that can be improved with practice. Knowledge is information that is acquired primarily through learning or direct exposure. Skills are acquired through experience and practice, although they may have started with learning.

Strengths lie in four main areas.

- Technical skills are needed to accomplish the tasks of our job. They are what we first bring to our role—especially early in our careers, and for many are always the primary focus of their work.
- Leadership strengths are those things that help move the business forward—especially as we mature in our careers, including strategic thinking, visionary leadership, innovation, and ability to deliver results.
- Management strengths are those interpersonal and organizational abilities that allow us to direct others, coordinate their efforts, and develop people and teams.
- Personal strengths are those attributes that create trust, commitment and enthusiasm, such as communication, conflict management, and relationship building.

Opportunities

Opportunities for growth are the converse. They are things that are difficult for you, either because you do not have talent, you haven't learned about them, or you haven't had enough experience with them. Identify the activities and experiences in your work life you have found particularly difficult or have received critical feedback on. In addition, are there skills or experiences that you are interested in or potentially good at, but have not been exposed to?

Values

Values are the underlying beliefs that you carry that help you make decisions about what to do at points of difficulty. Consider work, hobbies, relationships, a time of change, a decision you made, and a time of pride. Ask yourself why you did what you did—what principle led you to make the decision that way? Ask it three times, each time asking why to the preceding why.

Worksheet 2.1 provides a framework for identifying your values, which determine what you will or will not do. You can also download an editable version of the worksheet with a list of possible values at **www.BermanLeader ship.com/InfluenceandImpact**

Worksheet 2.1 Values Checklist

Values Exercise[viii]

Write down possible values or use values from the sources in the footnote. Circle all the values that resonate with you. Do not overthink it—just pick the ones that feel right to you. Then, combine those that are similar. For example, you might group Acceptance, Tolerance, Collaboration, Inclusiveness, and Patience. Then, pick a name for the group of values. That name could be one of the values, or a summary value.

Write down all the values that resonate for you, grouping them by how similar you see them. If you need additional circles, draw them. Then pick one value as a name for the group.

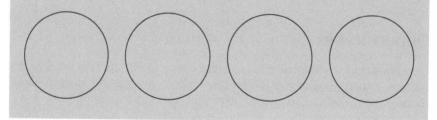

Preferences

Preferences are the things you choose to do or be exposed to, not because you perceive them as right or essential, but rather as sources of enjoyment and gratification. Also, think about what you enjoy doing from several different views. What do you enjoy from a task perspective? Doing tasks? Managing people?

Then think about what you like doing from a style perspective. Do you prefer planning, or implementing? Do you like working in teams or on your own? Do you prefer clear direction and explicit deliverables, or do you thrive on flexibility and responding to novel situations? Do you care about observable successes, or feeling gratified?

Preferences determine what you would like to do if you had the option.

Insight

People often feel that things like autonomy and decision rights are essential elements of their values—giving them up is like giving up a part of oneself. That makes it almost impossible to change their understanding of what they do. It's important to see that these things are more like strong preferences than values. Think carefully about what defines your personal identity—your values—and what is something you like to have or are accustomed to. We are not telling you what should or should not be integral to who you are. We do encourage you to consider the possibility that "artifacts," such as how you speak, what you wear, and how much authority you exert, may be only manifestations of an underlying part of your identity that can be demonstrated in a variety of ways.

Worksheet 2.2 provides a framework to help you clarify your strengths, opportunities for growth, values and preferences. Be as specific as you can. This is about concrete activities, not general styles.

Download an editable worksheet at **www.BermanLeadership.com/ InfluenceandImpact**

Insight

People come in packages. We are not built from a checklist where you get to pick different characteristics for different circumstances. As a result, our natural inclinations can be hugely helpful in some situations, and not as helpful in others. From a leadership perspective, people who are good at big-picture, strategic thinking often do not have the patience to closely manage project details to ensure on-time delivery. From a personality perspective, people who are very good at supporting and encouraging team members to grow and develop often struggle to provide direct, critical feedback to underperformers. Our character is not our destiny, but it takes substantial time and effort to be what Rob Kaiser calls a versatile leader— someone who can demonstrate different characteristics in different contexts.

Worksheet 2.2   SOVP Analysis: Strengths, Opportunities, Values, and Preferences

	Strengths				Opportunities for Growth			
	Talents	Knowledge	Skills	Experiences	Talents	Knowledge	Skills	Experiences
Technical/Business								
Leadership								
Management								
Personal								

	Values	Preferences
Technical/Business		
Leadership		
Management		
Personal		

Examine Your Mental Models

While you do not have control over all aspects of your job, you do have some control over what you prioritize, how much effort you put in, how you do what is expected from you, and most importantly, what you feel about the work you do. Cognitive psychologists have found that we have control over how we feel, by changing our mental models and by changing our behavioral repertoires.[ix]

What are mental models? They are the heuristics, or rules of thumb, that you develop over time, that help you sort through and manage the enormous amounts of sensory information we collect every day. Some theorists call them scripts or plans.[x] We have simple mental models for objects or categories, as well as more complex scripts for activities, roles, relationships, and emotional situations.

For example, if I said I ate at McDonalds for lunch, you automatically know that I either used a drive-up window or walked up to a counter, ordered my food, paid for it and then had it delivered to me on a tray. You also may automatically make judgments about my lack of concern for my diet.

Imagine if you have no information as to what type of restaurant a McDonalds is. You could not tell, without walking in, whether you were going to a fast-food restaurant or a fancy steak restaurant. How should you dress? When do you pay? Do they serve alcohol? Now, imagine if this were true about every store or building you walked into, car you drove, office you worked in, person you talked to. Daily life would be completely exhausting.

We have a variety of mental models of what the workplace, or an individual job should be. We have scripts in our minds about what a manager-subordinate relationship should be like (or even if it should be called that!). We have scripts for what lunches are like at work, and different ones at home. What are your pre-existing assumptions for your job, for your manager, for your colleagues?

Define Your Mission

An essential part of understanding how to develop your influence and impact is clarifying not only what you do well, but also why you do your job. Like many of the areas for self-assessment in this we are suggesting a midpoint between a psychological deep dive and a superficial checklist.

Your mission flows from three questions: Who or what needs me? What do they need and why? What must I deliver to meet those needs?

Most of the time, you do not choose your personal mission. It is given to you.[xi] Not in the sense that someone says, "This is your mission." Your mission usually emerges from outside you, whether you are on your own, the CEO or the founder of an organization, or simply an employee. Typically, it is defined by needs—either your needs or someone else's. Sometimes those others give you a mission. Sometimes you have to figure it out yourself. Either way, finding your mission is a journey of discovery.

> *Richard and Michelle Laver's story about the development of their nutritional health company Kate's Farms Komplete Shakes is a case in point. Their daughter Kate was born with cerebral palsy, which made eating normal food out of the question. As Richard explained to George, "Michelle and I decided it was time to take matters into our own hands to try and alleviate Kate's symptoms and together we tried to find the most holistic ingredients we could so that our daughter would start feeling better."*

Many people define their mission by developing systematic ways to solve a problem shared by many others. That's exactly what Richard and Michelle did, assembling resources and then building distribution step-by-step to establish a business. At every step of the way, they've kept a picture of Kate front and center—in the company's name, on their website, in their minds and hearts.

Your mission statement is intended to help you understand the major driving themes in your life, and how they shape the choices you make, the activities you engage in, and the ways you feel satisfied. Use Worksheet 2.3 to identify some of these themes, and how they shape the choices you make, the activities you engage in, and the ways you feel satisfied.

Begin by identifying the things that you do or have done. Don't just focus on right now but pay attention to the things that you have done that take a large part of your life. These should primarily be action verbs, like "work," "write," "play golf," "play with my kids," and the like. Try to be specific. Instead of saying "work," say "manage people" or "write press releases."

For each one of these, indicate what purpose each activity serves, in the short run. For example, if you say, "play golf," then the why could be "to relax," or "to spend time with friends" or "to build my skills" or whatever the short-term reason might be.

Then think about what the long-term goal is for one or more of these. In the case of golf, it could be "to balance my life" or "to maintain relationships." The long-term goals may apply to more than one of the things you do.

What themes emerge from this? Are there consistencies across the kinds of things you do? Are there things that particularly excite you? Is there an overriding long-term theme(s) in what you do? Turn these themes into a sentence or two, to describe what is really important to you.

Worksheet 2.3   Define Your Mission

I DO (Activities)	IN ORDER to (Short-term goal)	SO THAT (long-term goal)
1.		
2.		
3.		
4.		
Recurring Themes:		
Mission Statement:		

Download an editable worksheet at **www.BermanLeadership.com/ InfluenceandImpact**

Examine Your Long-Term Objectives

Last, consider your long-term objectives. Think five to ten years out (any further out and who knows what might happen to you). Stand in your future and consider what you want it to be like. Consider your professional life and your personal life, as these are tightly intertwined. Then, look backwards and see if you can see how you got here.

Your objectives will invariably impact the choices you make. If you need to stay in a certain location for personal reasons, for example, think about growth within the US instead of in a global company. At every point in the process, you should be thinking about whether your strengths, motivations, values, preferences, and objectives match. You may feel that you have a good sense of these before you start. Or you may feel that these are too removed from the practical job at hand. Either way, go through this exercise, and open yourself to these questions: "What matters to me now? What will matter to me over time?"

The Solution, Step 3. Do the Job Needed the Most

Adrián was a mid-level partner at one of the top law firms in the country, and had the potential to become one of the most senior partners in the firm. He worked well with his team, and mentored both his direct reports, and many junior people in the firm who sought him out. As a result, his reputation among the non-partner staff was extraordinary. As one respondent said, "He's fantastic—people view him as an asset—someone who really cares about them."

His manager, however, wanted Adrián to focus on longer-term, strategic business. "He has to find a way to whittle away the noise. . .and focus on client development," he said. "Adrián needs to ramp up his presence and his big-picture thinking."

Adrián felt stuck. As he explored these reasons with his coach, he realized that he was not really clear on what was expected of him as a partner. As he thought about this, he spoke about his father, who had never achieved his own potential due to post-traumatic stress disorder. This created conflicts for Adrián—he felt that the more he succeeded, the more it distanced him from his family.

He reached out to colleagues and his own mentors to make sense of this. What did the firm want him to focus on, and what was interesting to him but not absolutely essential? He began to open up his schedule so that he could spend more time with clients, thinking about how to expand the practice.

Adrián continued to talk about his feeling that he wasn't "The type of person who becomes a partner at this firm." As he began to do the things that partners do, however, he began to realize that he deserved to be partner, and built his self-confidence and self-assurance.

To be clear, we are not telling you to wear a smile and go along with whatever the boss says. We are also not saying you should just "put your head down and do what you are told." It is very clear from research[xii] and experience that business outcomes are better when people are free to speak up, identify issues, solve problems, and generate new ideas. What we are saying is that to be successful you need to understand the larger context of your job, which shapes your current job requirements. Then, decide if the job you have is the job you want to be doing. That is the first step toward building your influence and impact—understanding the context of your role.

Key Takeaways

You've got this. To improve your influence and impact generally requires a mindset change to: 1) Accept your situation as it is currently, including all the emotions that come with not being in control of your job; 2) Rediscover your value by assessing your own strengths, opportunities for growth, values and preferences, and mental models; 3) Apply yourself to the job needed the most.

End Notes

[i] Joseph, T. M. (2011). "The psychological contract: What is missing? What is next?" *Journal of Psychological Issues in Organizational Culture*, 2(1): 67–75.; Rousseau, D. M., Hansen, S. D., & Tomprou, M. (2018). "A dynamic phase model of psychological contract processes." *Journal of Organizational Behavior*, 39(9): 1081–1098.

[ii] De Meuse, K. P., Dai, G., & Hallenbeck, G. S. (2010). "Learning agility: A construct whose time has come." *Consulting Psychology Journal: Practice and Research*, 62(2): 119–130; Eichinger, Robert W., & Michael M. Lombardo. (2004). "Learning agility as a prime indicator of potential." *People and Strategy*, 27(4): 12.

[iii] Ross, L. (1977). The intuitive psychologist and his shortcomings: Distortions in the attribution process. In *Advances in experimental social psychology* (Vol. 10, pp. 173–220). Academic Press.

[iv] Briggs, Katharine C. (1987). *Myers-Briggs type indicator*. Form G. Palo Alto, CA: Consulting Psychologists Press.

[v] Owen J. E., Mahatmya, D., & Carter R. (2017) Dominance, influence, steadiness, and conscientiousness (DISC) assessment tool. In Zeigler-Hill, V., & Shackelford, T. (eds), *Encyclopedia of personality and individual differences*. Springer, Cham.

[vi] Hogan, R. (2020). "How to build Hogan assessment systems." *Consulting Psychology Journal: Practice and Research*, 72(1): 50.

[vii] Cattell, H. E. P., & Mead, A. D. (2008). The sixteen personality factor questionnaire (16PF). In Boyle, G. J., Matthews, G., & Saklofske, D. H. (eds), *The Sage handbook of personality theory and assessment, vol. 2. Personality measurement and testing*, (pp. 135–159). Sage Publications, Inc.; Prewett, M. S., Tett, R. P., & Christiansen, N. D. (2013). A review and comparison of 12 personality inventories on key

psychometric characteristics. In Christiansen, N. D., & Tett, R. P. (eds), *Handbook of personality at work*, (pp. 191–225). London: Routledge.

[viii] Gustafsson, H., Lundqvist, C., & Tod, D. (2017). "Cognitive behavioral intervention in sport psychology: A case illustration of the exposure method with an elite athlete." Journal of Sport Psychology in Action, 8(3): 152–162.

[ix] Thornton, M. A., & Tamir, D. I. (2017). "Mental models accurately predict emotion transitions." *Proceedings of the National Academy of Sciences*, 114(23): 5982–5987.

[x] Abdel-Raheem, A. (2020). "Mental model theory as a model for analysing visual and multimodal discourse." Journal of Pragmatics, 155: 303–320.; Mandala, S. (2017, November). Talk in the mind: Scripted dialogues and mental scripts. In *Dialogue Analysis VII: Working with Dialogue: Selected Papers from the 7th IADA Conference*, Birmingham 1999, (22): 357.

[xi] Bradt, G. (2013, November 26). Why You Don't Get To Choose Your Mission. It Chooses You. Forbes. Retrieved February 7, 2021 from https://www.forbes.com/sites/georgebradt/2013/11/26/why-you-dont-get-to-choose-your-mission-it-chooses-you/?sh=3016a43a221b

[xii] Frazier, M. L., Fainshmidt, S., Klinger, R. L., Pezeshkan, A., & Vracheva, V. (2017). "Psychological safety: A meta-analytic review and extension." *Personnel Psychology*, 70(1): 113–165.

PART II

The Solution: Discover Your Levers of Influence

CHAPTER 3

Discover the Essentials of Your Job

Collect the Data

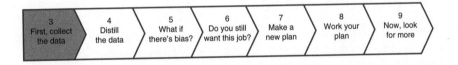

3 First, collect the data	4 Distill the data	5 What if there's bias?	6 Do you still want this job?	7 Make a new plan	8 Work your plan	9 Now, look for more

"It does not do to leave a live dragon out of your calculations, should you live near one."

—J. R. R. Tolkien

The first step in enhancing your influence and impact is to gather information so that you can say with confidence what you need to do and how you need to do it to demonstrate your value to the organization. This is a three-part repeatable process you can use throughout your career. First, identify the essential sources of information. Find out who are your stakeholders, collaborators, team members, and managers whose points of view contribute to your success. Second, collect what overt data you can by formal interviews, casual conversations, and requests for feedback. Third, observe those people and teams in the organization to understand the implicit behaviors, symbols, underlying assumptions, and fundamental

41

beliefs. Watch what managers respond positively to, and what they ignore. Attend to who is successful, and who is not.

Your risk of having emotional reactions to the data you are collecting is less because it is not about you—it's about your organization or your job. The risk is still there, however. Your objective at this stage is to collect the data without judgment and without confirmation bias. As you collect the information, try to maintain your emotional balance, particularly when you disagree with or are unhappy with the information. Right now, you want to learn as much as you can, so that you can later analyze the data and draw useful conclusions that will help you be your best self.

Know Your Business

It is essential to understand the organization's priorities. Senior executives have access to business strategy and organizational plans, so can easily identify many of these answers. Individual contributors and middle managers may have to rely on published materials, company website information, and town hall meetings.

Mission, Vision, and Values

Begin with the organization's vision, mission, or purpose. Some companies have all three on their website or their quarterly reports; some have one; and others you have to discern it from what the owners and leaders say. If you work for a public company or not-for-profit, they may have these on their website, or in their annual report. Many healthcare organizations print their mission and values on posters or plaques and display them prominently. Other companies do not have anything visible. Keep in mind there is no standard definition of mission, vision, and values. What you are looking for are broad statements of why the organization is doing what it is doing.

Business Strategy

Understanding the business strategy is relatively straightforward at the organizational level. The business strategy determines the critical areas of focus for the organization as a whole. For you, regardless of your level, your strategy is tied directly to your manager's, and your 2nd level manager's objectives and goals. Their critical areas of focus most relevant to you are your objectives.

Michael Porter's Monitor Group suggests there are two fundamental elements to any strategy, whether it is at the organizational level or a single team: Where Play, and How Win. Where Play is all about deciding where you should focus your attention, since you cannot focus on everything. How Win is all about what differentiates you, your team or your organization from everyone else who does what you do.

Different functions, business units, and divisions may have different priorities. For example, as an organization Apple focuses on the higher end of the market, and its unique selling point is design. The business as a whole is geared to out-innovating their competition, with designers as the ultimate heroes. Apple Stores, however, are all about service. Apple Stores' focus is the retail customer experience, and what differentiates them is the knowledge and helpfulness of their personnel. Their real job is to create loyal customers. For them, it is all about service.

Oskar, a board member with a private equity firm referred Dana to Bill as a coach. Dana had been an absolutely engaging individual since he joined the company two years before. He did a great job of reenergizing the company and providing strong inspirational leadership. Dana had encountered some serious headwinds recently. By mid-Q4, it was clear that revenues and cash flow were significantly lower than what was needed. At this point, the board became much more deeply involved; which, as you know, is not ideal. There were two areas of focus. First, Dana's leadership team was not where it needed to be. Second, the commercial team was consistently missing their targets.

Dana had spent the majority of his career in commercial roles, and successfully turned around an underperforming division of a conglomerate. He saw lots of low-hanging fruit at the current organization, and took on the role using ". . .the philosophy that has served me well."

As Bill and Dana discussed the business, Bill asked, "What is the private equity firm's exit plan?" As Dana considered this, he noted, "I thought I had a few more years, but they seem to be in the process of getting out of many of the B2C assets." Dana had an aha moment. He continued, "Maybe I only have 12 to 18 months, not three years. That means I need to focus on the tactical, day-to-day activities of the sales force, and make sure I have a team that is 100% focused on the other issues. But that de facto makes me senior vice president of Sales, doesn't it? That's not what I signed up for."

Dana vetted this realization with several of the PE advisors, as well as all of the members of his leadership team. The feedback was consistent: Focus on commercial success for the next 12 months. He hired a supply chain leader and leaned on his heads of marketing and finance. Almost immediately, Dana brought revenue, bookings and free cash flow up above target. As a result, the PE firm received an attractive offer to purchase the company sooner than anticipated, and they began working on the details of the sale process.

During the due diligence process, the board chair pulled Dana into some of the work that was supposed to be done by a consulting firm. He began to work on the details of the presentation to the potential acquiring company, but quickly pulled back. "This isn't my top priority," he declared, in a meeting with the consulting firm. "My priority is still making sure we are positioned to sell, not to sell myself. I need you to improve what you have for market landscape and the growth opportunities, and revise the financials to reflect the results we are delivering."

The company was sold nine months after Dana realized his job was not what he thought it was. And, not only was Dana able to successfully sell the company, but he was also the only person asked by the new owner to stay on the management team. And after leaving, he took on another CEO role where he continues to be successful.

Worksheet 3.1 provides a template to help you outline the business and functional strategies. Using this approach, you will get reasonably close to understanding what the critical areas of focus for your function and department are.

Download an editable worksheet at **www.BermanLeadership.com/ InfluenceandImpact**

Know the Organizational Culture

Standing at the top of an organization looking downwards, culture is a broad description of the way people in organizations think and act. At more granular levels it can be incredibly complicated. Edgar Schein, one of the preeminent thinkers about organizational culture, defined it as "the pattern of shared basic assumptions—invented, discovered, or developed by a given group as it learns to cope with its problems of external adaptation and internal integration—that has worked well enough to be considered valid and, therefore, to be taught to new members as the correct way to perceive, think, and feel in relation to those problems."[i]

The manifest culture of the organization (not the aspirational culture that is represented by corporate values and prescribed leadership behaviors) can be understood at three levels.

First, there are observable actions, behaviors, and ways of interacting that make up what Schein called "the artifacts of the culture." Examples of this can include the physical layout (Environment), the ways of communicating (Relating), and management of decision-making and conflict (Behaviors).

At the next level, there are the articulated Values and Attitudes that underly the artifacts. These can be thought of as heuristics or rules of thumb that people use, which show up in day-to-day life as the artifacts. We sometimes refer to these as operating principles, such as "Quality first" or "Bias to action."

Finally, there are the underlying assumptions—sometimes conscious and intentional, sometimes implicit—about individuals, groups, and organizations

Worksheet 3.1   Business and Functional Strategies

Overarching Corporate Strategy:
Focus Areas for the Corporate Strategy:
Strategic Focus Areas for Your First Team, Department, Function or Unit
Strategic Focus Areas for Your Main Team, Department, Function or Unit
How can You Help Achieve those Focus Areas? (Work and Cultural)
What are Your Top Three Priorities in Delivering the Needed Outcomes?

that are referred to in the cognitive science literature as mental models or schemas.[ii] What makes a schema cultural is that it is held and adhered to by most of the organization. It is also reinforced by the organization's approach to rewards and recognition.

Strategy and culture interact to define the norms, behaviors, and relationships in the organization. And, as we noted earlier, the cultural norms can vary to some degree at different levels of the organization. For example, an organization may endorse open conflict resolution, but a single manager or team may discourage that.

Worksheet 3.2 provides a set of ratings you can use to describe both the culture of the organization in general, and your manager and team specifically.

Worksheet 3.2 Cultural Dimensions

These dimensions are derived from both George's work on Brave Leadership,[iii] and Erin Meyer's The Culture Map.[iv]

Behaviors			
Discipline:	Consistency	1 2 3 4 5	Flexibility
Feedback:	Indirect/Supportive	1 2 3 4 5	Direct and Blunt
Disagreement:	Private or Avoidant	1 2 3 4 5	Open and Direct
Decision-Making:	Authority-based	1 2 3 4 5	Consensus
Relationships			
Communication:	No shared references	1 2 3 4 5	Many shared references
Authority:	Rank/Experience	1 2 3 4 5	Merit
Relatedness:	The Individual	1 2 3 4 5	The Collective
Trust:	What You Do	1 2 3 4 5	Who You Are
Attitudes			
Strategy:	Consistency	1 2 3 4 5	Innovation
Process:	Rules-based	1 2 3 4 5	Results-based
Focus:	Internal	1 2 3 4 5	External
Time:	Rigid	1 2 3 4 5	Flexible
Values			
Growth:	Error-focused	1 2 3 4 5	Strength-focused
Equity:	Inclusion	1 2 3 4 5	Meritocracy
Results:	Results First	1 2 3 4 5	People First
Prioritization:	Timeliness	1 2 3 4 5	Quality
Environment			
Layout:	Private	1 2 3 4 5	Open
Office Decor & Dress:	Formal	1 2 3 4 5	Casual
Facilities:	Spartan	1 2 3 4 5	Indulgent

Derived from George's BRAVE model described in *The New Leader's 100 Day Action Plan*, this framework helps you identify your organization's artifacts, such as behaviors and interpersonal interactions, as well as the underlying attitudes, expectations, and assumptions. You can use the worksheet by asking others what they think, or by simply observing the organization and answering the questions on the worksheet based on your own perceptions and judgments. The former will give you a more complete picture, but the latter will be faster and less obtrusive.

Download an editable worksheet at **www.BermanLeadership.com/ InfluenceandImpact**

Know Your Manager(s)

Your ability to influence others, and impact the organization, is greatly influenced by your manager(s). In the quote at the beginning of this chapter, your manager is "the dragon." As noted in Chapter 1, when you are aligned with them, everything is easier.

Ask the Right Questions

Given their importance, data gathered from your manager should be a top priority. Start by asking the right questions directly. What was I hired to do? What do you need and expect from me? Also, ask about their job: What are their responsibilities? What does their manager expect from them?

Make sure you ask *how* you should do your job, as well as what you should do. For most managers, how the two of you work together—your ways of working—are the details that make the difference. How do you want me to communicate with you? How should I keep you informed? How should I disagree with you?

It never hurts to ask, but bosses (like other relationships) may not tell you what matters. They may have idiosyncrasies and not recognize them. They may be self-conscious about their preferences or may think they are one way, when in fact they are different.

Observe Your Manager

Pay attention to what your managers do as well as what they say. In team meetings, what do they pay attention to? How do they handle disagreement? In 1:1s, when do they probe, challenge, and dig into the details and when do they listen and then move on? When preparing for their own presentations, what do they prioritize and what goes to the back of the deck? This will give you clues to what the most important priorities are for your manager (and your manager's manager).

Zach was the general manager of a division of a consumer products company. He was bright, insightful, and strategic. He prioritized what made the business successful. He had enough P&L experience and management training to know that he had to focus on gross margin and annual operating contribution as well as revenue growth. He built a strategic plan that was not just about the numbers; it addressed several other aspects of the business, including supply chain issues and quality management. He became increasingly frustrated, however, because his manager seemed distracted most of the time. In their one-on-ones, he was often distracted by email. He skipped over Zach's presentations in team meetings and seemed bored by the things that Zach knew were important to business success.

Zach became increasingly annoyed, feeling that his manager was unfocused, lacking insight, and disrespectful. He also knew that his manager was becoming increasingly annoyed, giving Zach negative feedback for not being a team player and not buying into the culture. His emotions were getting in the way of seeing a solution.

Zach began to observe his manager in meetings: What did he talk about? When was he paying attention and when was he distracted? When did he probe and question his team, and when did he move on quickly?

When he reported back at the next session, Zach explained, "It has become very clear that he only cares about sales. Not even revenues— he's only interested in new orders coming in. Every time someone talks about issues like supply chain, raw materials, or quality, he zones out. But our metrics include Earnings Before Interest and Taxes (EBIT) and Annual Operating Contribution (AOC)—we won't be successful if we don't focus on these other things as well." He continued, "I get it. He came from sales. That's where he has worked most often."

Zach reflected for a moment. "He thinks my job is sales. Nothing else. He probably knows that the other things matter, but he has no expertise in them. He focuses on the thing he knows more about than anyone else, doesn't he?"

Based on this insight, Zach focused 90% of his time with his manager on sales-related issues: Customer allocations, pipeline review, building customer relationships, and the like. He spent the remaining 10% on the other issues, and made it clear he "had it handled" and didn't need any input. Within three months, their relationship had improved, Zach's feedback was substantially better, and the manager even took him out to dinner. Ironically, six months later Zach's manager was let go, because the division was hitting sales numbers but had missed on all measures of profitability.

There are a wide range of areas that matter to managers. Some of the most important ones are:

1. Priorities, including what they are expected to accomplish (results), and what they care about personally (wins)?

2. Metrics, including how they evaluate success (yours and theirs), and what their most important quantitative goals are?

3. Communication, such as mode, manner and frequency, and whether you communicate to others directly or through them?

4. Decision-making: Who makes what decisions, and how collaborative it should be.

5. Disagreement, including whether, where, and how to disagree.

Worksheet 3.3 provides you with sample questions to both ask and observe your manager. Your goal is to figure out what your boss wants from you, and how they define their own job. What they want you to do, rather than what you want to do. Remember, it is not really about you. Often it is about your manager, or their manager.

Download an editable worksheet at **www.BermanLeadership.com/ InfluenceandImpact**

Tip for Leaders

When you move to an executive-level job, the expectations of your manager change. For directors, and even VP-level managers, helping your people grow and develop is a part of the role. They are there to help people think through ideas and develop plans. But, by the time you get to be a vice president, your manager (usually the C-suite of a division or the company) may not have the time to help you think or solve problems—they expect you to do the thinking and give them well-considered, fully analyzed options to help them make a decision.

One of George's clients had what he called a 90-6-4 rule that clarified decision-making for his team. That client had joined a company as CEO and explained to the entire company that he expected:

- them to make 90% of the decisions. These were all day-to-day decisions that kept things moving forward. Of course, as CEO he was ultimately accountable for all operating decisions, but they had to make them, and he had to support them.

- 6% of decisions to be shared. They would discuss, debate, and decide together.

- 4% of decisions were his to make as CEO. And, just as he would support the 90% of decisions that everyone else made, he expected them to support the 4% of decisions he made.

Worksheet 3.3 Questions for Manager (Answers and Observations)

1. What is my job?
a. What are your most important priorities?
b. What are my most important priorities?
c. What can I do differently to make our team really successful?
d. How will you evaluate me? The team?
e. What is mine to decide? What is yours to decide? What is shared decision-making?

2. How do you like to work?
a. Do you prefer finished products or works in progress?
b. How much detail do you want—high-level, or fine—when I am proposing a plan?
c. How should I disagree—in private or in public?
d. What is the best way for me to keep you up to date on my progress?
e. What's your preferred mode, manner, and frequency of receiving communication from me?
f. Do you prefer scheduled meetings with agendas, or informal drop-ins/phone calls?

3. What should I be doing?
a. Is it more important to deliver on commitments versus achieve the ultimate goal?
b. Do you prefer incremental improvement or bigger, bolder change?
c. What's the right balance between: Big-picture strategic work versus detailed execution?

Insight

There is a big difference between expressed wants and unexpressed underlying needs. It helps to understand why people feel the way they do. Think in terms of three Whys deep—that you either ask directly or try to ascertain. Ask: Why this matters, then What that does for them, then Why that matters. Ask: What that does for someone else, then What that does for someone else, then What that does for someone else. Keep asking until you understand the context for your job and its direct and indirect impact on others. It is always helpful to understand how people are trying to meet their basic needs for things like security, autonomy, respect, belonging, etc.

Know Your Stakeholders

Identify Your Stakeholders

Identify who your key stakeholders are. You have people in your direct line—above you are your manager and your manager's manager, below you are your direct reports, and their reports (we usually refer to them as skip-level reports). You have people in your indirect line—people you work with but who are not in someone else's organizational "tree." You have suppliers—people who provide you with ideas, information, or material whom you depend on. And you have customers: People who depend on you for ideas, information, or material. Worksheet 3.4 is a Stakeholder Map that you can use to identify these people. Map them out. Determine who would have a point of view on what your job really is. Make sure you identify a wide range of stakeholders, including your boss' boss, boss' peers, your peers, boss' influencers, suppliers and customers. Once you have identified them, go one more degree of freedom out. You can always cut back, but you do not want to miss essential players at this early stage.

> *José joined his new firm from a fast-moving, deal-focused organization. He was accustomed to having a great deal of autonomy, and was able to focus on his specific responsibilities. After six months, his manager pointed out that decision by consensus was the norm in their organization, and that on several occasions a single person was able to delay a decision simply by expressing concern about a minor downside risk.*
>
> *Based on this feedback, José and his coach created a stakeholder map. He then asked his manager for feedback. She identified over a dozen other individuals whose involvement would be essential for various types of business move. Although José did not really understand why these people had an opinion on his decisions, he acquiesced, spent time engaging with these other stakeholders, and listened to their concerns. He quickly realized that this made his decision-making more straightforward and productive.*

Download an editable worksheet at **www.BermanLeadership.com/ InfluenceandImpact**

Worksheet 3.4   Stakeholder Planning

Put the names of critical stakeholders in the graph. The closer you put individuals to the center of the circle (you), the more frequently you work with them. Those farther away from the center may be less frequently seen, but can be critical to your success. The four sections are designed to help you identify stakeholders in a broad sense who can impact your success.

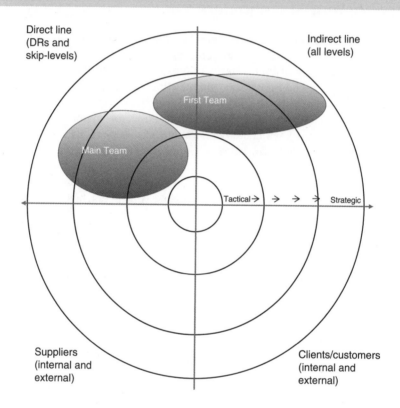

Ask the Right Questions

Find the time to talk to your stakeholders. Ask them what they think is critical to your job. What do they think is important for you to know? What do they see as the deliverables of your job? Where are the important dependencies? What are the obstacles in terms of people, resources, structures? How should you do your real job? How is information communicated? How do you motivate others? What are the political dynamics in the organization you need to understand? The questions from Worksheet 3.5 can be used to understand your stakeholders.

Download an editable worksheet at **www.BermanLeadership.com/ InfluenceandImpact**

Do not expect any of them to have the whole right answer. Each person will have some observations and points of view, but these are not facts and truth. With your stakeholders, you are seeking more input than direction. Make sure

Worksheet 3.5   Stakeholder Questions (Answers and Observations)

1. **What is my job?**
a. What are your most important priorities?
b. What are my most important priorities?
c. What can I do differently to make our team really successful?
d. What are the most important metrics you evaluate me on? The team?
e. What does our shared success look like?
2. **How to form a group?**
a. Tell me about what you and your group do best?
b. Where do you need the most help?
c. What do you think is important for me to know—especially as it relates to your group?
3. **What should I be doing?**
a. Where are the important dependencies?
b. What are the obstacles in terms of people, resources, structures?
c. How should we communicate?
d. What are the political dynamics in the organization I need to understand?

to get their perspective on organizational norms, mores, and operating principles, and about your team/function/business unit. Ask about the same areas you looked at for yourself about the culture: How do people tend to interact? How do they handle conflict? How are decisions made and kept? Where do they focus their attention—big picture, or small details?

Trusted Colleagues   There is a subset of your stakeholders we call trusted colleagues. They may show up in all levels of your stakeholders, but they serve specific functions.

Seconds are internal people who are explicitly assisting or supporting you. If you are uncomfortable with some of these questions, or the people you want information from, your seconds may be able to ask the questions for you. They may also be able to gather information that people are reluctant to tell you directly. A coach or internal mentor may fill this role for you.

Informants are internal people who observe what is going on in other parts of the organization and tell you about it. These are people, often former employees or more junior people you have gotten to know, who can provide a

Know the Criteria You Will Be Assessed On

Guest Contributor: Ben Dattner, Ph.D.

As the end of each calendar or fiscal year approaches, many organizations conduct formal performance reviews and provide feedback to employees. These appraisals often involve individuals being assessed in comparison to aspirational "competency models" and include criteria such as "Leveraged business acumen to drive execution" or "Identified opportunities to innovate and develop new processes or practices." However, most competency models don't take organizational reality into account; instead, they evaluate people as if they were working in some kind of abstract utopian ideal, rather than in a specific job in an actual workplace. In addition to challenges in creating and utilizing consistent criteria to evaluate and provide feedback to people with widely diverse kinds of jobs, it is also difficult for organizations to provide people joining the organization with an accurate sense of how they will actually be evaluated, often because the truth about what actually matters in the company isn't what it should be.

As fans of *The Office* know, there is a large gap between rhetoric and reality in corporate America; which, depending on one's perspective and personal career situation, can either be comedic or tragic. In order to succeed in a new organization, it's crucial to understand what actually constitutes good performance in the judgment of those who will be evaluating you and others. As discussed in this chapter, it's helpful to consider how key stakeholders define and evaluate success both in terms of the "what" of results and in terms of the "how" those results are achieved. Knowing the "real" criteria for success, in practice rather than in theory, is necessary both for the self-assessment of one's own performance, as well as for evaluating others *in a manner that is consistent and congruent with the organization's culture.* It can also be helpful to ask trusted colleagues with experience in the company to alert you to any gaps between the company's "official" success factors and what actually matters. Sometimes organizations clearly state that they want to hire iconoclastic innovators who will speak up and push back on their superiors or resist groupthink, but those who try to do so might find out that this stated value is more aspirational than actual. Asking others about lessons they have learned from surprises or misunderstandings can help you identify cultural taboos, without having to break them and learn the hard way.

flow of information from the ubiquitous back channels. Look for people who are willing to tell you what they think is true, regardless of their self-interest. You may not agree with what they say, but you know it isn't self-serving.

Scouts are external people with different perspectives. They could be customers, former employees, or mentors. They can tell you what they see (the artifacts) but they won't necessarily understand the underlying assumptions of the organization.

Observe Your Stakeholders

Just as you observed your manager's behaviors, tone, and body language, observe your stakeholders to understand their perspective. Use the same questions you asked of your stakeholders and watch for clues to the answers. In this case, remember that you have to consider who they are to you, and what their needs and objectives are. In structured 360° assessments, we have learned that peers tend to rate people lower than other rater groups. Moreover, your stakeholders may have less information, because they only see you occasionally or in specific contexts.

Stakeholders can teach you more than anyone else about "elephants in the room."[v] These are issues in the organization that everyone knows are there and no one wants to bring up. You have to decide whether to ignore the elephant, defer it, discuss it with others to find paths around it, or confront it head-on.

If the issue is a matter of ethics or legality, you have to find some way to address it, or risk being scooped up in the problem. Alexander Butterfield's role in the Nixon White House is a case in point. Despite doing what he thought was the right thing, he had difficulty finding work and struggled to maintain his otherwise good reputation.

Occasionally the issue is like a myth: It is likely untrue but has taken on a life of its own. In this case, asking questions like, "Why do we do it this way? Have we ever considered alternatives?" is enough to get people to look

---

Insight

How you deal with feedback, both positive and negative, is critical to this process. Remember, people have two typical reactions to criticism. The first is to focus in on the most negative feedback and defend, explain, contextualize, and otherwise qualify or invalidate in some way. The second is to respond, "Well, that is their perception." Remember that your objective is to focus on the synthesis of all the feedback, not individual responses. Oftentimes, the most negative feedback is similar in content to the more constructive feedback; it is a matter of degree more than content. Of course, you have to consider the source of the information, but remember we are trying to understand the what and the how of your job, not you as an individual.

at the issue from a new perspective. Alternatively, if this issue is not mission-critical, you may choose to leave it for another time, when it becomes more of a problem.

Conclusion

You have amassed a lot of data, from multiple sources. Hopefully, you did this without making a lot of judgments and filtering data along the way. Take the time to go back through the data and find the essential themes and patterns that will tell you what you need to do more of, less of, or differently. You are almost there—one more step to identifying both the mission-critical priorities and the unwritten cultural rules associated with your role. Once you know enough to start acting on these, your influence on your manager and your team will increase, your impact on performance will grow, and you will be able to demonstrate your value to the organization. Most importantly, you have not had to change who you are—you have simply found what is needed for you and your organization to rediscover your value.

Key Takeaways

Discover the essentials of your job. Collect the data on your business, the organizational culture, your managers and other stakeholders including trusted colleagues.

End Notes

[i] Schein, E. H. (1992). "Defining organizational culture."(pp. 490-502) In Shafritz, J. M., Ott, J. S., and Y. S. Jang, Y. S. *Classics of organization theory* (3rd ed.). Pacific Grove, CA: Brooks/Cole.

[ii] Schank, R. C., & Abelson, R. P. (2013). *Scripts, plans, goals, and understanding: An inquiry into human knowledge structures.* Hove, UK: Psychology Press.; Paoletti, J., Reyes, D. L., & Salas, E. (2019). Leaders, teams, and their mental models. In *Leader*

Thinking Skills: Capacities for Contemporary Leadership, 277–306.; Schmidtke, J. M., & Cummings, A. (2017). "The effects of virtualness on teamwork behavioral components: The role of shared mental models." *Human Resource Management Review*, 27(4): 660–677.

iii Bradt, G. B., Check, J. A., & Lawler, J. A. (2016). *The New Leader's 100 Day Action Plan* (4th Ed). Hoboken, NJ: John Wiley & Sons.

iv Meyer, E. (2014). *The Culture Map*. New York: Public Affairs.

v Bradt, G. (2013, August 7). How Leaders Can Address the Elephant(s) In the Room. Forbes.com. Retrieved February 7, 2021, from https://www.forbes.com/sites/georgebradt/2013/08/07/how-leaders-can-address-the-elephants-in-the-room/?sh=55c1eb9a5660

CHAPTER 4

Now Write Your Working Job Description

The Essential What and How of Your Role

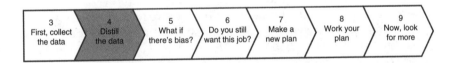

"No one should be ashamed to admit they were wrong, which is but saying, in other words, that they are wiser today than they were yesterday."

—Alexander Pope

Y ou have collected a wealth of data about yourself, your job, and your organization. In truth, there is more information here than you can use. Our next task is to sort through the data and condense it to a clear, straightforward description of what you now know is essential to your job. That framework, which we call your working job description, should explain:

- What drives our work? What matters to the organization? To the owners?
- What are the norms, rules-of-the-road, and operating principles? How do people interact, make decisions, allocate resources?
- What is your manager responsible for? How are they evaluated?
- What does your manager need and expect from you? What can you expect from your manager, based on your data?
- What do your stakeholders need from you? What do you need from them?
- What is your working job title, which accurately describes your responsibilities, independent of what your organizational title is today?
- What are your essential priorities?
- What do you need from your team? What does your team need from you?

Keep in mind, you are not trying to figure out, "What did I do wrong?" Where you are now may well have been the right choice based on the information you had at the time. The context changes, the players change, and the strategy and priorities change. Reframing your job to what is expected and needed now, and will be needed in the future, is both reasonable and appropriate. If you take 100% responsibility for shifting your priorities and your methods to do what is needed in the job now, you are likely to have at least 50% more influence and impact than you have today.

Alternatively, you may realize that you are struggling because what is expected and needed by your organization does not fit with your strengths, values, and interests. This will lead to the big decision you have to make in Chapter 6: Do I stay and commit? Or do I look for something different? First things first: What is the situation today?

Take One More Look Back at the Beginning

Before you start down the path to a new, more impactful understanding of your role, you should take a step back one more time to get a clear view of your assumptions and expectations going into this job, so that you understand not only what your current state is, but also why you have made the choices you made. Don't overthink this, as it's important that you spend more time on what you've learned from collecting the data.

When you accepted your job, you had a mental model of what your job was going to be. Think back on what you were expecting and consider the following domains. Recall what drew you to this job, and this organization. Ask yourself whether the organization has changed, or the job has changed, or your manager or team has changed, or you have changed.

The Motivation

Why did you want the job? What was your motivation? Most likely you wanted to do good things. Everyone has a balance of three goods: Doing good for others, doing things they are good at, and doing good for themselves. Which of these three was most important to you in choosing this job? Were you drawn to the organization's mission—doing good for others? Did you think it leveraged your strengths particularly well—doing things you're good at? Were you excited about the compensation or potential recognition or another aspect of doing good for yourself? There is no right answer here. It is useful to understand your motivation for taking the job.

> ⇒ *Has your motivation changed? Are you still driven by the mission? Are you learning and growing? Are you getting the compensation and acknowledgment you need?*

The benefits   When you started, what did you anticipate would be the personal and professional benefits of the job? People look for different things in their jobs, and companies offer different psychological benefits, both intentionally and structurally. For example, a well-established, conservatively run insurance company is likely to offer security and stability, while a fintech start-up will offer challenge and growth.

> *When AT&T was split up into the "Baby Bells," they changed from a single, highly stable workforce with great benefits based in the suburbs of NYC, to seven smaller, more nimble and risk-taking businesses that had to move quickly to re-establish their positions. However, many of the legacy employees were both trained and predisposed to being risk-avoidant and reliable corporate citizens. As a result, staff turnover increased dramatically, as legacy employees could not adapt to the needs of the new environment.*

> ⇒ *Have the benefits you were looking for changed? Have you changed what benefits are important to you?*

The Expectations and Responsibilities

People refer to expectations in a variety of ways. What is the organization asking you to accomplish and what is the intent behind that request: What will happen next after you've completed that? What did you think you were there to do and get done? How did this fit within the larger organization? Was there a job description? Did the job have clear expectations, authority, and accountability?

For example, what authority did you think you were going to be given? Typically, there are two types of authority: "Strategos" is the art of the general—arranging forces before the battle. "Taktikos" is about arranging forces in the battle. What did you expect to be told, and what was your purview to decide, either alone or with input?

> When Neville Isdell was group president of Coca-Cola Europe, his strategies were crystal clear. At subordinates' meetings with him he was always fully supportive of choices they made within those strategies. And he was equally clear about redirecting them when they tried to move outside the strategic boundaries.

⇒ **What were you supposed to be responsible for? Did you have the resources needed to be successful?**

The Relationships

How did you think about your relationship to your manager? Your manager's manager? Your peers? Your team? What were you expecting to get from them, and what did you think they would expect from you? These underlying assumptions of you and your colleagues contribute to the work experience, for both managers and team members, when they are not aligned.

> Sharon had explained to Ellen what she expected in training presentations to the HR team, and how the organization liked PowerPoint decks to be structured. Sharon gave her a template, and made it clear the template should be followed.
>
> The next presentation, however, did not follow the template and as a result was not well received. When Sharon asked Ellen why she hadn't followed the template, Ellen replied, "Oh, I thought it was just a recommendation. I thought the ideas would be communicated more effectively with a different type of deck." When Sharon explained that, as her manager, Ellen should expect to follow her directions, Ellen was nonplussed: "I thought you would want the benefit of my point of view," she replied.

⇒ **Have your relationship expectations changed since you took this job?**

The Accountabilities

What did you think you were accountable for? How would you be evaluated, and was that a fair judgement of your work? Did you know what your manager meant by "accountability?"

> *John Michael Loh, United States Air Force Air Combat Command during the first Gulf War said: "I used to believe that if it doesn't get measured, it doesn't get done. Now I say if it doesn't get measured it doesn't get approved . . . you need to manage by facts, not gut feel."*

⇒ **Have the standards of performance, time expectations, and results of successes and misses changed?**

Summarize the Data

How do you sort through all the data you have collected? Start with the end in mind. The endpoint of this exercise is to write your working job description, including the objective, subjective, and implicit aspects of your role.

Once you have collected the data about what your organization really needs from you, turn this information into insight: A cohesive understanding of your work situation that will enable you to decide if you still want the role, how you can build your influence and impact. You may need to make several passes through the material, distilling and synthesizing it until you have both a clear understanding of what your current state is, and how you get to your future state.

You cannot possibly do everything that all of your sources have recommended. Some of what they have said is idiosyncratic to them, and sometimes there is good reason for not doing what they recommend. Some perspectives are weighted more than others, for example. The challenge of this step is to understand and summarize the *most consistent* and *most important* feedback and recommendations, so that you can set clear priorities for yourself.

Worksheet 4.1 is the template for the working job description. In this worksheet, you lay out the job title that most accurately describes what you are expected to do (Your Working Job Title); why your job exists (The Mission); what is the job needed (The Deliverables); who it involves (The Stakeholders); how you should best do it (The Cultural Norms); how you should work with your manager and their direct reports (Your First Team) and your own direct reports (Your Main Team); and what success looks like (The Future). For each of the areas of your job description, consider both your manager's view, and your stakeholders' views, and create your own synthesis.

Some parts of your working job description will be consistent and obvious: Deliver net new sales; conduct a marketing campaign; upgrade the corporate website. Different stakeholder groups may have identified different objectives. In addition, the information should have pointed to behavioral expectations and attitudes, such as, "Make sure your manager looks good" or, "Build alignment as broadly as possible." Make sure to include the interpersonal and political recommendations (what some people unfairly refer to as "Soft Skills").

The Mission

Start with why the position exists—your mission. This should capture the problems you need to fix or the opportunities you can take advantage of. Look at things that would not happen right without you and your team in the job. For example, Dana's 'why' (from the private equity case on pages 48–49) was to set the company up to be put on the market.

The Deliverables

Your deliverables are the endpoint of the views, opinions, and expectations of four groups: The business, your stakeholders, your manager, and your team. We will examine each of these in order.

As we noted in Chapter 3, understanding the business' needs includes understanding the needs of owners and investors. What you pay attention to depends on whether the company is publicly traded, owned by private equity, or closely held by a family or small group. In the case of the former, you should be able to understand their needs based on either analyst information or their quarterly and annual reports. For the latter two, Chapter 3 helped you to identify the mission, vision and business strategies to some degree.

At the same time, observe the owners' and the C-suite leaders' behavior. What do they do with profits? Is there profit sharing? Do adult children of the owners work in the company? Do family members retain jobs they would not have in the open market? We are not making value judgments about these questions. We simply want to clarify that some of the decisions made by "the business" are based on individuals' needs and objectives, rather than the business objectives per se.

Lay out what you and your team should deliver—your objectives/goals/outcomes. Objectives are general. Goals and outcomes are specific. Together, they comprise what you are accountable for. For example, Dana needed to drive top-line revenue growth and have a management team and infrastructure in place that a prospective acquirer would value.

The Stakeholders

Who are your stakeholders? What are they responsible for? What are they looking for from you? Lay out organizational relationships, authority, and interdependencies. Capture members of your first team, members of your main team, and other stakeholders. Clarify what their relationship is to you: When you can make decisions, how you work interdependently with others, and how you influence them so that you both impact the rest of the organization—how others' work/lives will be made better by you and your team. What are their key priorities, and how can you help them achieve those priorities? When you think about what your priorities are, you cannot really say, "I'll meet my person X's priorities and not meet customer' Y's priorities." You have to find a way to try to meet both. This can be very complicated, and at times can reveal significant conflicts among stakeholders.

David was a vice president of Logistics in a pharmaceutical firm, reporting to the executive vice president of Manufacturing. David was responsible for distributing pills to pharmacies all over the country.

The company had created new blister-pack packaging to reduce loss and ensure the pills' quality. They planned a national launch with extensive advertising and prescriber meetings.

Just as the blister-packs were being sent, it was discovered that the packaging was too thick, and many people could not push the pills out of the pack. The only way to fix the problem before the launch was to dramatically increase production up-cycles and pay overtime and increased materials fees for higher-quality materials. Doing this would create problems for the manufacturing group, as it would put them significantly over margin targets.

On the other hand, sales leadership clearly indicated that the pharmacies and prescribers would not work with the product as currently designed, as there were safety issues associated with patients not being able to access the medication easily.

David had to make the decision—do I do nothing and risk sales missing their targets, or do I repackage the drugs, and interfere with manufacturing targets? Who was more important, his solid line manager or the commercial organization?

David solved the problem by focusing on the customer, and fixed the blister-packs. But he still was graded down by his manager that year.

The Cultural Norms

Dig into the ways you need to act in order to deliver the objectives/goals/outcomes. Consider the critical cultural themes like collaboration, conflict, communication, and hierarchy. What are the underlying beliefs and values of the organization that you need to attend to?

It is just as important to understand how the organization wants you to do the job as it is to understand what initiatives and tactics you need to take on. How you do your job reflects both the culture of the organization, the culture of the team, and the preferences (or should we say idiosyncrasies) of the manager. As we discussed in Chapter 3, there are a wide variety of dimensions that help to make sense of an organization, your manager, your stakeholders, and your team. This will help you decide "How" you should behave, interact, and engage with your environment. Of course, each company, team, and manager can have unique expectations for the "How," so be sure to add in any that seem to you to be recurring or particularly important.

How you interact   How you communicate and what you communicate varies widely from person to person and organization to organization. How you handle conflict is enormously significant: Doing it wrong can derail you incredibly fast. The quality of relationships, including level of formality, degree of deference, and use of rituals all shape the culture. The structure and process of meetings is usually organization-wide.

How you behave   We noted earlier a range of behaviors that are particularly relevant to your working job description. How decisions are made can be highly specific to your manager and your own management style. How, when, and how often to communicate are also specific to individuals. What metrics are used, and what priorities are emphasized, can be manager-specific or established for the organization. Psychological safety depends on the individual manager, but organizations have ways of working that transcend individual leaders.

Values and assumptions   Organizational attitudes and assumptions about autonomy and collaboration underlie many of these behaviors. Attitudes toward workers' drive and motivation do as well. Beliefs about inclusion, and the importance of diversity of approach and thinking, can determine many behavioral artifacts. Other assumptions also show up in a variety of specific behaviors, including the importance of quality versus timeliness, data versus intuition, and form versus function.

Your Manager and Their Direct Reports (Your First Team)

You have collected data on what your manager thinks is important in terms of business results and personal wins, and what their manager thinks is important.

You asked, "What am I doing particularly well? And, what should I be focusing on that will make me even more effective?"

At the same time, you asked what they need and expect from you.

And, you should have observed your manager and your first-team peers (manager's direct reports): What do they focus on? What catches their attention? What are they responsible for, and what do they need? You may want to look at things that would not happen right without them in their job. What is their role, responsibility, breadth, or priority change? What does their manager pay attention to?

Darlene was responsible for e-commerce for a new set of customer-focused security solutions. She devoted her efforts to capturing the customer acquisition flow from initial contact to sale. Her approach was highly technical and was confusing to many of her colleagues who were less schooled in digital analytics. She knew, however, that her manager, the general manager of one of the business units, was himself a highly analytic, metrics-focused individual. Her skip-level manager, the CEO of the company, would look at very granular data if the results were not on target.

Darlene understood that she needed to provide her manager with the metrics to support the growth plan required by the private equity firm that owned them. She provided weekly updates of data at each step of the prospect chain, what the cost of acquisition was, and what the revenue projections were. As a result, Darlene was always able to get her manager's attention. Her manager clearly trusted her and gave her comfort that she knew what was taking place in her business. Within two years she was promoted to be general manager of a small business unit.

Your Direct Reports (Your Main Team)

Teams vary widely in terms of their knowledge, skills, and styles. They also have different experiences. In this self-analysis, synthesize what you have learned about your own team. Are they a real team, with shared responsibility for results, or a workgroup of individuals who are independent, but may share some processes? Do they need close supervision, or is that just your preference? Who needs structure, and who needs flexibility? Who needs support, and who needs to be pushed harder to excel? For example, a team that has had an interim manager, for several months will likely chafe at the notion of close supervision. In this example, you may need to limit your own need to "trust but verify" until the team has accepted that you provide added value and are not devaluing what they have done on their own.

Stand in Their Future

Finally, think about what your stakeholders would say in 18 months, when someone asks how you are doing. What would make those stakeholders say, "Wow, what an amazing person. They are one of the best people I have worked with (or for)!" Try not to think about it from your point of view. Think about each of them and the data you have collected. What are the most consistent themes that they would say has made you so invaluable?

Turn this into a statement for yourself, so you can clearly articulate what the people in your organization want and need from you. This is what will build your influence and impact. This is your picture of success.

Your Working Title

You have learned that your job may be somewhat different than you thought it was. One thing to consider is, given what you need to be doing, what should your working title be? We aren't suggesting you change your formal title within your organization. But if you consider what a more accurate title would be, it may help you to hold on to the focus and priority that you are setting.

As one executive recruiter put it, "I don't look at the titles on an organization chart—especially in an evolving organization. I look at the boxes as problems to be solved or opportunities to take advantage of. My job is to fill those boxes with people with the required strengths, motivation and fit."

Remember the case of Dana in Chapter 3, who adopted the working title of SVP of Sales and Executive Recruiting. In spite of his formal CEO title, he was directly responsible for, and hence the leader of, those functions.

Even though you're going to think through your working title last, put it at the top of your worksheet as it's the organizing concept for everything else.

Download an editable worksheet at **www.BermanLeadership.com/Influence andImpact**

Worksheet 4.1   The Working Job Description

Category	Description
Working Title (do last)	
Working Mission	
Critical Deliverables	
Cultural Norms	
Key Stakeholders	
How to Work with My Manager and Their Direct Reports	
How to Work with My Direct Reports	
The Future	

Evaluate the Working Job Description

Most people tend to focus on what is most important or most gratifying to them. You may be gratified by focusing on what you find most fulfilling in your job. But unless what is gratifying to you also meets the needs of your boss or organization, you may be swapping internal achievement for external success. If salary increases, increased responsibilities, development opportunities, and promotions matter to you, balancing what you find valuable with what your organization needs from you the most will be much more satisfying than focusing exclusively on doing your own thing.

Your working job description is not a replacement for the job description that human resources maintains. It is intended to identify and emphasize the most important business-focused and culture-focused elements of your role. The goal is to create a clear understanding of what excellence looks like from the outside, so that you can make the changes that will enhance your influence and impact.

Once you have created your working job description, you may want to share this document with your manager and other key stakeholders for their input.

While your responsibilities are going to be different in different areas, focus on the most important, most mission-critical aspect of your job and figure out if you are a sponsor, leader, manager, doer, or facilitator.[i] These roles largely determine your accountabilities.[ii]

Key Takeaways

Write your working job description—the essential what, why, and how of your job. This is not the same as your organizational job description. This one includes your working title, accountabilities, stakeholders, cultural norms, how to work with manager and their direct reports, as well as your direct reports. It should include a future vision of what success looks like.

End Notes

[i] Bradt, G. (2020, July 7). The Difference Between Deputies and Chiefs of Staff. Forbes. Retrieved February 7, 2021 from https://www.forbes.com/sites/georgebradt/ 2020/07/07/the-difference-between-deputies-and-chiefs-of-staff/#37532032119f

[ii] Bradt, G. (2016, February 16). Accountability: The Essential Link Between Empowerment and Engagement. Forbes. Retrieved February 7, 2021 from https://www.forbes.com/ sites/georgebradt/2016/02/16/accountability-the-essential-link-between-empower ment-and-engagement/#5e690ffc2a4a

CHAPTER 5

What If Bias Keeps You from Being Effective?

Increasing Influence in Difficult Contexts

Contributing Author: Greg Pennington, Ph.D.

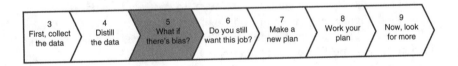

| 3 First, collect the data | 4 Distill the data | 5 What if there's bias? | 6 Do you still want this job? | 7 Make a new plan | 8 Work your plan | 9 Now, look for more |

S omething just happened to you. It may have been one or more of the following things. Someone called you Pat, though your name is Lynn. You
offered a contribution to a team discussion that was met with silence just
before someone offered a strangely similar contribution that was met with head
nods and affirmations. Instead of getting the performance and development
feedback you expected, the feedback was surprisingly critical or frustratingly
void of suggestions for improvement. Your feedback seemed even more critical when compared to others whose performance numbers seemed subpar
compared to yours, and others who at least received constructively critical

feedback. You were offered a role with expanded responsibility, it came with an interim title, though you were convinced that someone took on a similar role with what appeared to be the same experience but with a permanent title. Once you were promoted to VP your administrative assistant asked if you had ordered your company car—which no one had mentioned.

Do organizations discriminate? Yes. Individuals and leaders do so as well. Is it against you? Perhaps. If there is a need to make a choice between one person and another, you have to somehow identify a difference and make a decision. If you are working to reach a higher level in an organization, there are fewer opportunities than there are candidates, and decision-makers have to discriminate between one candidate and another. The question would not be whether or why discriminate, it would be why me? Why us? Why now? It is important to recognize that there is a need for an organization to make decisions that differentiate one choice from another. It is also important to recognize that discriminating between individuals and groups is different than discriminating against a person or a group.

Knowing what the organization wants and needs is a critical component of being an effective leader. Deciding what you are willing to give up to be a part of the organization is a critical personal decision. Asking for what you want is an option with accompanying personal and professional risks.

We are often alternating between an integration about what we know, think and feel in general and what we know, think, feel and wonder about specific situations. Even if you believe there is a high probability that an organization discriminates against a defined population, the question for us in this chapter is whether this particular organization is discriminating against you.

Because you are wondering whether you want to invest your time, effort and other things, like your identity, you want to know both what is true, as well as what choices you have in response to it.

How would you test any hypothesis regarding discrimination? The first question is, "Is it me?" You need to know if you are qualified and doing what you can to control the things you can. The second question is, "Is it my boss, my peers, my team?" The situation may be more individual if they approach others unlike you in the same way, or if they approach others like you in the same or different ways? The third question is, "Is it the organization?" One source of data is how people like you are represented in all areas and at all levels. Another is whether the successful people like you are seen as exceptions to the rule (for example, not like those other Blacks, or more like a man than a woman).

There is data to support the impression that something is likely to serve as an obstacle against Black American leaders, specifically in corporate organizations. A recent Korn Ferry study based on interviews of 500 corporate P&L leaders identified five headwinds.[i] The significance of investigating a population of P&L leaders is to test the assumption that when you are able to measure results, the value of other variables of discrimination are reduced. "I delivered the goods, I hit my numbers. That's all that should matter!"

There are five related approaches leaders can take to address what may be experienced as unfounded, unfair, overlooked, or stereotypic dimensions of categories of differences. Though the strategies are presented as discrete options and in a specific sequence, it is more accurate to consider them as an interrelated, sometimes coordinated, sometimes not, array of strategies or areas of focus. The areas of focus to consider are: (1) Calibration, (2) Information, (3) Demonstration, (4) Negotiation, and (5) Transformation.

Keep in mind that the complexity of any situation increases the likelihood that multiple explanations and some interplay of a variety of strategies are at play.

Calibration   The primary emphasis in calibration is to find a way to validate what you are experiencing by comparing it to other reference points. These include other experiences of your own and comparisons to experiences of others. It is primarily an internal process and provides a foundation for the other areas of focus. The power of calibration is in how it influences your framing of the situation and your personal responsibility for it.

Information   The focus on information emphasizes the importance of gathering additional sources of data and broadening the context of your experiences. It also provides perspective about individual, leader, and organization patterns and impacts. It is a shift from a primarily internal process to one that is external in its accumulation of data and in its sharing of data. The power of information is in how and with whom you share it.

Demonstration   The focus on demonstration is an emphasis on proving you can perform at a level expected of you by the organization. It is also an effort to eliminate the possibility that others and the organization can use failure to perform as a justification for discrimination between and/or against you based on that variable. Demonstration is an external process, and its power is convincing yourself and others that you are willing to be judged on the essential need of the organization to deliver results.

Negotiation   The emphasis of negotiation is leveraging the areas of calibration, information, and demonstration to align what the organization needs and wants with what you need and want. It is clearly an external process and certainly an interactive one. The power of this area of focus is in connecting changes in behavior to observable outcomes.

Transformation Transformation represents the fifth area of focus and emphasizes the opportunity for you as a leader to change others and the organization. It takes advantage of the degrees of influence accumulated through the previous stages. As both an internal and external process, it derives its power from you being genuinely committed to changing others, being in a position of interpersonal and organizational influence to do so, and effectively engaging others in the process.

Let's walk through examples of leaders utilizing each of these areas of focus.

Calibration

This first area of focus is a relatively low-risk strategy when viewed in terms of how the organization might react to your efforts. This focus on calibration includes a tremendous amount of self-reflection. It covers cross-checking your experiences with others in a variety of dimensions including dimensions of difference. Does this happen to all new employees, to everyone who is assertive? Does my manager challenge everyone in the same way? Does it only happen to women, or people of color? Is it more likely to happen to one group compared to another?

Something happens that causes me to pause and wonder what happened? You will see in the following case that it took a while at significant cost to calibrate her experience with other credible reference points. It seems simple when you are not the one involved, but it can be extremely difficult to ask the critical question, "Is what happened to me something that happens to others like me?"

Ann wanted to build her own company in the heavy construction industry. She knew at the time a female in the construction business would be rare. She also knew that success in any business was significantly determined by the effort one was willing to intentionally direct to that success. She put in the effort. When she failed to get awarded a contract, she put in even more effort. She worked the technical parts of the process and increased her time and efforts to build and leverage the relationship drivers for success. Each time she failed she increased her effort, taking full responsibility for her successes and failures. As her business became stagnant and then plummeted, her efforts remained steady but her explanation of success and failure shifted from a confident "I can do this" to a self-defeating expression of "Maybe I am not cut out for this."

Ann did not believe the construction industry discriminated against her on the basis of gender. She ignored the data that suggested the odds were against her. She failed to direct enough energy and efforts to getting feedback about how her experiences compared to those of others on the key dimension of gender. Ann was also so committed to being solely judged on her merits and results that she refused to see or believe that there may be other explanations. She trusted what she had always relied on would continue to yield the same results they had in the past. If she worked hard, she succeeded. If she failed, it was because she had not worked hard enough or was not capable. Ann grew more and more frustrated and then depressed.

You will see in Ann's story that there is a risk of not calibrating. However, overlooking the real obstacles in the environment can result in wasted effort, and you as a leader unfairly criticizing your own performance and underlying capability.

Eventually, Ann found a reference point in another woman—a peer—who served as a sounding board. She listened to Ann and challenged her belief that the only thing that mattered was results. She also supported her. Asking the question, "Does this happen to others like me?" is critical. Asking it of a credible reference source is essential.

Information

The second strategy or area of focus, information, is a bit riskier for you because it involves gathering data about discrimination and presenting it to someone else. One of the key questions in this approach begins with "Are you aware of. . .?"

Byron was a member of the executive leadership team in a business unit of a global manufacturing enterprise. He believed he had a realistic perspective about what he could and should take responsibility for. He was also sure about what still remained as unnecessary obstacles based at least in part on the fact that he was a Black American male.

Byron had also worked in all three of the business units. A consistent theme in his feedback over the years had been that he was too direct and intimidating, a common piece of "feedback" to Black men. It often included that he was not as sensitive as he needed to be to the teams he inherited, coming across as pushing for solutions before understanding the problems or their history. He was also considered to be trying to move too fast to turn things around. Byron felt, justifiably, that he was not fully supported by his current manager. Though Byron held several different roles as he moved from one business unit to another, they included interim assignments and were primarily lateral moves.

When he raised questions about his current role and previous roles, including about his relationships with his managers, he considered it to be an obvious matter of how he could become a member of the "good ol' boys." He also wondered what influence his race and direct style contributed to his sense of not being fully utilized. Byron devoted substantial effort to identifying what he did and how it contributed to how he was perceived and how his performance was assessed. It was still important for Byron to understand how his experience could be explained in a broader context. He was clear that gathering information and insight would help him appreciate the probability of his changes in behavior having a positive impact on his current situation and overall career.

Byron had access to multiple sources of information gathered over years of experience in the company. They included a widespread network, both within and outside the company. The information he gleaned was that there were key career-accelerating assignments that contributed to some decisions. He knew he had to be intentional about positioning himself for those assignments. He also learned that there were differential inclusion rates of people of color in some businesses, along with different rates of succession and retention.

Byron also recognized the need to continue taking ownership of charting his career path. That decision was relatively low-risk. He also saw both an opportunity and a risk in sharing his information about differential rates with human resources.

Byron eventually took an overseas assignment, based on information that global experience was one additional variable in decisions made. It also moved him out of a line of business that he was convinced had a weak track record of promoting persons of color.

Demonstration

Curtis was one of three likely successors to CEO. He was the only Black American. With degrees from Ivy League undergraduate and business schools, and repeated successes at a preeminent management consulting firm, Curtis had built his career through increasingly expanded finance roles in Fortune 100 companies.

When I met Curtis and worked with him, he was serving as CFO for a Fortune 100 company and was openly considered as one of three likely successors to the CEO and company founder. The chair and the board were reasonably transparent that Curtis and the other business presidents were comparable candidates to become CEO. At one juncture, Curtis understood why the board wanted him to run one of the major lines of business in order to demonstrate responsibility and capability for a major Profit & Loss center. Curtis accepted the role and challenge and performed well.

While Curtis was in this role one of the other candidates issued what was perceived by the chair and board as an ultimatum: "Make me CEO or I am likely to leave." He was given the role, quickly failed and left the company. The other candidate struggled in his business, while Curtis' business continued to perform reasonably well.

Soon after the first candidate had failed and left the company, Curtis pressed the question of whether he was now the leading candidate. He was told his business was not considered to be performing well enough to separate him from the other candidate based on performance alone, and there may be value in him attending a Harvard Executive Education program. Curtis left that meeting and said aloud to no one in particular: "What does a Black man have to do to be CEO here?!?"

His frustrated comment was overheard by a peer, shared with the SVP-HR and the CEO, and over the course of several closed-door discussions, became a point of significant concern. Key stakeholders, influencers and decision-makers wondered among themselves: "I did not know he felt that way"; "Would he be the right choice?"; "Is it always going to be about race with him?"

I asked Curtis about his hallway comment and the ripple of conversations it stirred. He said:

> No Black person gets to this level in corporate America without recognizing there is a Black tax to pay. You are better off assuming you have to do more than others to even be in the game. Every now and then, you get frustrated and need to call it out. Once I did that, I was back on track. Yes, I should not have said it out loud and yes somebody should have asked me directly what was going on. Bottom line, one way to deal with all of this is to overperform.

Curtis eventually became one of the few Black CEOs of a Fortune 100 company. Curtis and others would consider this a happy ending. He and other Black senior leaders of major corporations still reflect on what they could have accomplished without the headwinds and extra hurdles they encountered along the way.

Do organizations discriminate against people of color and women by asking more of them? The research suggests yes. The individual stories remind us that the experience is real. What power or influence do you have to address this expectation, this discrimination, that sets the performance bar higher for some than for others?

Simply stated, if you know there is a tax, as Curtis described it, you can decide to pay it. Once you become a tax assessor or tax collector, you may have a different degree of power or influence you can use to change the formula.

Negotiation

Nigel was convinced that his boss was discriminating against him. Nigel led a global wealth management fund that generated significant profits to the investment bank and exceeded expectations each year. He had moved steadily upward, and with expanded responsibility in the financial institution was at least on a par with his peers. He understood, and explicitly acknowledged and accepted, that being one of the first of his color in every role meant that he had to exceed expectations to counter any doubt others had of him. He needed to focus on his performance in order to mitigate the propensity for others to undervalue his results. Nigel still insisted that he was not fully accepted and that he was likely to always be treated differently because of his skin color. The fact that he was the only person of color in his group further solidified his belief.

I asked Nigel if he had tested his assumptions. I also asked if he would share what still convinced him he was being discriminated against and what difference it made to him now and in the future. This is how Nigel answered:

> *When we meet as a team, the senior partner of the group greets each of us by name. "Good morning Jim." "Welcome Tom." But he usually greets me by saying "What's up Slick?" I let it wash over me the first few times, but since it kept bothering me, and he kept doing it, I asked if he noticed how he greeted me differently from others. He said "Yes. Is there a problem?" I responded, "Yes, it bothers me. Why do you do it?" He said it was because of the way I dressed and that it shouldn't bother me. I replied, "I don't think I dress any differently than others. I would prefer you call me by my name." He insisted he didn't mean any harm by it and told me I should not be so sensitive. I knew then that he was not going to change. I wondered how many times he would think that anything I achieved was because I was "slick!"*

Nigel left the company two weeks later to join a competitor. His judgement was that either the company or his boss had some need to discriminate, and that he had few chances for success in this organization. When asked a few weeks later about his decision to leave, Nigel shared that he felt he needed to make sure he had done all he was willing to do to make the situation at least tolerable. He had deliberately confronted his manager with how he felt, and wanted to know what his manager was willing to change in his behavior. Nigel thought and felt that once he had made a clear offer and request, and his manager had refused to offer any changes in return, there was nothing left to negotiate.

It is not uncommon for leaders in organizations to act surprised that employees decide to leave the company. They may also exclaim that if they had known the person was a retention risk, they might have been able to convince them to stay. It has also not been uncommon in my coaching of Black executives for them to wonder whether they had done all they could in the area of negotiating before they decided to leave.

Transformation

Melvin was on the high potential list for a large public utility. His next step was to become an officer of the corporation. Having spent all of his professional career in the industry, he understood and accepted that he would find himself in roles and situations in which he would likely be one of the first or few. Having grown up in a working-class family and being the first in his family to graduate from college, Melvin had close ties to the community in which he was raised.

Throughout his career Melvin was adamant about doing things in a way that was true to how he saw himself. He was smart, analytical, direct, results-driven, sometimes intimidating, and a Black male. At this point in his career, under consideration to become an officer, he was stuck because he felt in taking this next move, he would have to become less Black. His family and friends back home seemed to confirm his fears, suggesting he would have to sacrifice that part of his self-identity in order to fit in the role and expectations of a corporate officer for a public utility.

Melvin's transformation included testing his assumptions about what he would have to sacrifice. He realized that he had been steadfast and true to himself as he navigated his career. He also recognized that conscious and unconscious instances of bias may have contributed to him exaggerating some of his behaviors. He was able to sort out when his behavior was driven by a need to prove his decisions were right and when it was driven by a need to improve a decision. While Melvin wrestled with how to integrate his self-identity and corporate identity, he also understood that at this next level he would have additional influence and power to make a difference in how the organization managed diversity.

Melvin ultimately retired as president of a major utility. He took pride in the Black leaders and employees he mentored in overt ways, and many others he had sponsored out of the spotlight. He was true to his directness in using the power of his position to demand more diversity in recruiting sources and set high expectations that candidate and succession slates included diverse candidates. When asked directly how he had reduced the headwinds for other Black employees and leaders, he also noted how he had helped shape a peer circle of other black American leaders in the company, across other businesses, and in several professional associations. In recognition of his family roots, he referred back to traditional assertion that "to whom much is given, much is expected in return." There is a responsibility that comes with power and influence.

* * * * *

You have taken your share of responsibility to calibrate your thoughts, feelings, and reactions to believing you are being discriminated against. You took another step to not only gather additional information but to also share and use that information to help others remove blind-spots and better appreciate the impact of their behaviors on fully utilizing all their available resources. You went further to demonstrate that you could meet and exceed the explicit and implicit expectations others had of you, and used that level of performance as a basis for negotiation about what you were willing to do and what you would ask of others. You may have also found yourself in a position or role in which you were able to focus on the transformation of yourself, colleagues, peers and others, and even the broader organization, to make changes.

Throughout all of this you may still have found yourself believing the organization continues to discriminate against you. Along the way you may have exercised appropriate legal options. Whether you have felt or seen any progress at any point, you always have the option of leaving. If what the organization really needs and if what really matters to them most is to fully utilize all its resources, sometimes the spark that may ignite real change is the loss of one of those resources. You may be the person who puts a face to the fact that the organization is discriminating against valuable resources. Sometimes you may be the critical spark needed.

Key Takeaways

What if bias keeps you from being effective? Calibrate to validate the bias. Gather information to understand patterns. Demonstrate how well you can perform. Negotiate to align the organization's and your own needs and wants. Transform others and the organization as necessary, possible, and appropriate.

End Note

[i] Korn Ferry Institute. (2017). The Black P&L Leader: Insights and Lessons from Senior Black P&L Leaders in the United States. Retrieved February 7, 2021 from, https://www .kornferry.com/content/dam/kornferry/docs/pdfs/korn-ferry_theblack-pl-leader.pdf

CHAPTER 6

Now That You Know the Truth About What Your Organization "Actually" Needs from You

Do You Still Want This Job?

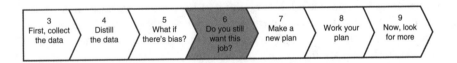

3	4	5	6	7	8	9
First, collect the data	Distill the data	What if there's bias?	Do you still want this job?	Make a new plan	Work your plan	Now, look for more

"I have respect for the past, but I'm a person of the moment. I'm here, and I do my best to be completely centered at the place I'm at, then I go forward to the next place."

—Maya Angelou

Y ou are now at a pivot point in this process. You have collected the data from various sources. You have spent time thinking about why you took this job and what you expected when you accepted. You have analyzed the information and condensed it into insights and understanding about where you are. You have, in the words of Jim Collins, "Confronted the Brutal Truth."[i]

Now, it is time to put these insights into action. There are three basic questions you need to answer. This may take a little time but it is simple in principle:

1. Do you still want the current job?

2. If yes, are you willing to commit to changing what you need to be successful and appreciated?

3. If no, do you want to stay with the organization you work for?

Before you do that, however, it may be useful to confirm some of our basic assumptions:

You can't go back in time. Everything you've done so far, good or poor, is in the past. Whatever your answer, nothing you have said or done implies you made a mistake or failed in any way. Spending time on recrimination is natural but does not help you move forward. And we are here to help you get to a place where you feel successful and appreciated. While it's important to learn the lessons of the past and their implications for the future, your job now is to choose how you're going to go forward from this moment in time.

Sunk costs are irrelevant. The time you have spent in the current job, and the successes you have achieved are valuable, but if you are feeling stalled or underappreciated, you should ignore the investment you have already made. Your objective is to make the right decision now based on the information currently available. Looking at how much work, or how much time you have devoted to your current job will not help you reach your longer-term objectives. If your past efforts and achievements give you something that you can leverage, great. But refocusing on the clarified job, and your own objectives now, will give you a greater advantage.

You are in charge of you. In most situations, you have a choice of what to do now. You can choose what to focus on, and you can choose how to think, relate, and interact with the people in your organization. Most people are not truly "stuck," with no options but to suffer through. Some certainly are, but in many cases, you can actively work to improve your situation, either by changing what you do in your job, how you approach your job, or by finding a job that fits with your strengths and your objectives.

The Pivot Point

The pivot point is your answer to the question, "Do you still want this job?" To answer the first question of whether this is the right job for you or not, you should consider three sub-questions that comprise the main question.

- Can you do this job as you have outlined it, *in this organization*? Does it align with your strengths?
- Can you influence others and operate effectively *in this culture*? Are you comfortable with the behaviors, artifacts, assumptions, and underlying beliefs of the organization?
- Does the job provide value or meaning to you? Do you care about the direct, indirect, and knock-on impact you can have?

If you answer "yes" to all three, and yes to the main question of whether you want the job, then you are ready to excel at the job your organization needs from you. This includes making a commitment to align with your manager and with your organization, and a commitment to yourself to change and grow. This is not a commitment to your organization, to be clear. This is a commitment to *yourself* to work in a way that has a meaningful impact on the organization and its mission.

If you decide in the next few pages that you do not want or cannot do the job, as you have outlined it here, you may want to jump ahead to Part IV, Plan B. Chapter 10 will begin the process of letting go of those sunk costs, and moving on to something better.

Can You Do the Work?

The work to be done in a job requires that you have what industrial/organizational psychologists call knowledge, skills, and abilities (KSAs) appropriate to the role.[ii] Abilities are the things that you bring to your role that are not easily taught. They are the equivalent of what the Gallup Organization describes as talents. Skills are the behaviors, thoughts, and responses that have been developed through training and experience.

Most people intuitively understand the difference between skills and abilities. This is obvious in sports; some people cannot make a free throw in basketball no matter how hard they practice. Others make it look simple. It is the same in all aspects of life. You can learn some skills, but without natural ability, you are limited in what you can achieve. Confusing talent and skill can be a significant problem when working in an organization. It is all about accepting what you cannot change.

> *Grant is a highly skilled, talented CFO. He has a grasp of numbers and spreadsheets that allows him to gain insights that others cannot. While he has more than 20 years' experience in finance, he has always shown a facility for data. Because it comes so easily for him, he does not understand why others struggle with it. He frequently becomes frustrated by others on his leadership team. "It just isn't that hard," he'd declare. "You just have to look at the numbers and you can see that we are on a downward trend." After a number of discussions, Bill pointed out that he struggled to write clear, direct messages to the finance group, and needed multiple practice sessions to present effectively. "Your colleague in marketing feels exactly the same about writing marketing communications as you do about spreadsheets. For him, writing 'just isn't that hard.'"*

So, when we ask, "Can you do this job?," we are asking if you have the abilities, skills, and knowledge required to succeed in this job?" If you don't have the innate talent, no amount of practice can make up for it. Review the expectations of your job from your manager's standpoint, and the organization's standpoint. You may have the KSAs required for the job you thought you were doing, but not what is required for the job you now understand you have.

Insight

Make sure to look at your current strengths, and in particular your generalizable skills. Generalizable skills are applicable in many different roles. They are less about a knowledge area and more about an ability, like problem-solving or analytic thinking. You may want to check your opinion with a trusted colleague. You can build knowledge by investing in learning. You can gain skill—both specific and generalizable—with experience. Both take time, however. Be sure you have the time to invest before committing to it.

Keep in mind that many jobs do not require a talent to be successful. Experience and training can blur the lines between skills and abilities. If you are not a natural public speaker, you can still take a job that requires public speaking. Many people have developed the skill needed to speak to large audiences and have acquired the experience to overcome public speaking anxiety. Even the best natural public speakers have to hone their ability through training and experience.

Can You Operate in This Organization and for This Boss?

To really excel in a job, you have to be able to do the job in a way that the culture—and specifically your manager—can accept and embrace. That means one of three things: Your preferences and the organizational culture are reasonably consistent; you are willing and able to adapt your approach to the culture of the organization; or (less often) you are able to persuade the organization to adapt to your style and approach. Inclusive management in organizations[iii] requires work on both sides—the organization needs to be open to different styles, and the individual needs to work to adapt to the organizational style. As we said earlier, taking 100% responsibility for your side in that equation will get you about 50% closer to where you need to be.

Survey research has found that as many as 60% of people leave their jobs because of their managers.[iv] Based on our experience, the percentage of bad managers and bad jobs is less than 60%, but certainly greater than 0%. Some "bad managers," however, are really a misalignment of your expectations and interests and those of your company or manager. Often, jobs appear to be unworkable because either you or your manager have not made your assumptions, beliefs, and expectations explicit, which leads to conflict and unhappiness. That does not make either of you bad, it simply means that you need to find a job or an organization that is better aligned to your values, needs, and expectations.

The documentary, American Factory,[v] illustrates a dramatic version of these misalignments of needs and expectations. In the film, a Chinese company establishes a production facility in a mothballed GM plant. They describe the tensions between Chinese culture and American culture with regard to work. While the Chinese managers view the Americans as sloppy and unmotivated, the Americans view the Chinese managers as autocratic, unreasonable, and condescending. In reality, both groups are operating within their own culture, and struggled to adapt to a very different set of underlying attitudes and beliefs.

The key question is: How do you know when the difference is culturally bound, or a response to differences in expectations or objectives, rather than a bad job or a bad manager you should escape from? How do you know when it is not about you, but really about where you have found yourself? The difference matters because of the process you go through, and the options you have to resolve the situation. If the problem is a cultural misfit or a difference in workplace expectations, you may need to adapt yourself, because your organization and your manager have no inherent reason to change. If the problem is one of bad behavior or ethics, then you may have to decide if you have a responsibility to do something about it, or just look for another job.

Focus on the differences and decide whether they are 1) Minor and manageable, 2) Complementary, 3) Challenging, or 4) Insurmountable.

Minor and manageable Minor differences are relatively easy to handle—especially now that you've made yourself aware of their existence. When they come up, look for ways to talk about them openly, or shift gears to adapt to the other person or the organization. For example, if you are a resolutely punctual person, you may find an organization that consistently starts meetings late to be frustrating. You can talk about this with your team to persuade them to change, learn to adapt to being late, or ignore it as a minor inconvenience. If you are looking for autonomy and your manager is a micromanager, you may need to tolerate the behavior until you can find another role.

Complementary Work hard to synthesize complementary differences: They should be sought and embraced. There is extensive research demonstrating that multiple differences—in thinking, in beliefs, in attitudes—produces better results than similarity in most situations.[vi] Inclusive teams are more likely to be high-performing, and more likely to make high-quality decisions. They often require the most time to establish ground rules and more communication early in the formation of the team to avoid misunderstandings and misinterpretation. But as long as the team shares the same commitment to the organization's mission, vision, and values, those differences can be beneficial.

Challenging Differences should be resolved quickly, lest they fester. These are typically related to how you and someone else, rather than you and the organization, think of yourselves. The differences show up as behaviors, but are held onto by you and your manager, or your peers, or another stakeholder, because they represent underlying attitudes and values that are believed to be core to the person's identity.

> At a southern US energy company, a newly installed senior executive calls out errors or what he considers to be poor performance in public meetings. His team, however, is accustomed to a more genteel approach. Their prior manager, who they had worked with for over a decade, only addressed performance issues in one-on-one meetings, and even then, he was circumspect. Despite discussing this behavior with the senior executive, and offering specific alternatives, he returned to this behavior repeatedly. When we probed the reasons,

it turned out he grew up in a home with a verbally abusive father and attended a military high school where public shaming was par for the course. Becoming aware that this behavior was a part of what he thought authorities should be made it easier for him to gain some control over it.

Many of these challenging differences deal with fundamental motivations like respect, security, control, and autonomy. They show up around handling conflict, debate and disagreement, loyalty, or being included or excluded.

Usually, the first step in handling challenging differences is to approach it as a problem to be solved, rather than *A PROBLEM*. Start by raising the issue with your boss. Sometimes the behavior is due to a lack of self-awareness, and once you point out the problem, the manager is willing to make adjustments. If they are asking you to do things you do not consider to be your job, raise it directly. See if you can negotiate a different set of requirements or resolve what you and your boss think the job entails, perhaps using some ideas from the negotiation section of Chapter 5.

These challenging issues are sensitive to the inherent power differential in a manager/subordinate relationship. As a result, convincing your manager to adapt to you is much less likely to be successful. So, ask yourself, how important is it to you to exhibit that type of behavior? Do you have to be able to tell your manager what you think, in public, regardless of how it might land? Or can you address the issue in private, so that they are not embarrassed by you? If you cannot or will not let go of the particular behavior, this challenging issue may become insurmountable.

At times the expectations or the behavior you encounter is so outside the norm that it is impossible to work around. In this context you will have to take steps to change the situation, before it becomes a toxic situation—much like the transformation section of Chapter 5. For example, frequent swearing, including swearing at other people, may be considered the norm in some organizations. In this case the problem is not just with your manager, but with how the organization operates in general. Working to change the system you are in can work at times, and is often gratifying when you can overcome the situation and make for a better workplace. It may take quite a bit of time and energy. And, sometimes trying to get the organization to operate differently can backfire and make you the target of others' ire.

If the problem is an individual rather than the organization, one option you should consider is discussing the situation with human resources. In the case of an individual who is hostile or abusive, you can even file an employee relations (ER) complaint. Large organizations usually have very clear policies about ER complaints. They typically involve independent investigations and often corrective action if the complaint is found to be valid. Start by talking with an HR business partner or HR generalist who can help you identify what options you have within the company policy. Even small companies and startups will typically take complaints of harassment or inappropriate behavior very seriously. Given the ubiquity of social media, one unhappy employee can create significant difficulties for an employer.

Insurmountable   There are differences that fall in the area of contradictory values or unacceptable behaviors. This usually creates a toxic environment. And they often emerge when the real mission, vision, or values don't match the stated ones. Consider the case of Volkswagen, and their emissions scandal.[vii]

> *Volkswagen had a clear set of expressed values, that included social responsibility, sustainability, a spirit of partnership, and volunteerism. When the CEO, Martin Winterkorn, set the audacious objective of becoming the largest car manufacturer in the world within ten years, he did not realize that their diesel engines did not pass the strict California emissions guidelines.*
>
> *According to Elaine Shannon of the nonprofit Environmental Working Group, "The company had deliberately installed a 'defeat device' in diesel vehicles sold worldwide from 2009 to this year (2015). The device was really a bit of software coding expressly engineered to spoof standard emissions testing instruments and evade the federal Clean Air Act and related state rules."[viii]*
>
> *Intentionally or unintentionally, the CEO conveyed the belief that Volkswagen had to meet his objectives by all means necessary— including deliberately miscoding the software to get around the requirements. Although we don't know for sure, we suspect engineers either had to leave the organization or engage in this conscious deception. Whether Winterkorn knew about this or not, he was the leader of the organization, and responsible for what took place.*

If you find yourself in a situation where your values and the enacted values of your company or your manager are fundamentally different, you should not think about whether you should change. We would encourage you to either be a whistleblower, if you believe the other's actions are unethical or illegal, or to find another job. Conversely, if you find yourself managing someone with very different values than you, move quickly to take action, as people's values are unlikely to change very quickly.

> *In a leadership meeting, one of George's colleagues said he was going to do something that was in direct contradiction to one of the organization's values. The colleague stood his ground despite making it clear it was not negotiable. I called him privately the next morning and he*

told me he was going to go ahead. I explained that if he was going ignore the request, he was going to have to separate from the organization. That was the last time I talked to him. By the end of that very same day, that colleague was out of the organization and I had called all the other leaders personally to explain why.

There are a number of behaviors and environments that fall into the category of a toxic environment. We have identified several of them below, although there are certainly others we have not yet considered. If any of these sound like your current situation, you may need to take action quickly.

- No matter what you do, your manager criticizes you. If you think the manager has credibility, the criticism will inevitably wear you down and undermine your confidence and self-esteem.
- Criticisms are personal rather than performance-based. Performance-based criticism is part of the work world. But criticisms about your character, or aspects of yourself you cannot change, are unreasonable.
- You are belittled or demeaned by others at work. Some people feel it is their prerogative to tell you that you are stupid, poorly educated, inept or in some way incompetent.
- Your boss lacks self-control. Managers are human beings, and they have emotions that they have to deal with. No one, however, should have to tolerate being yelled at, sworn at or have objects hurled in their direction.
- What your manager expects is unreasonable. Most people have to work late at times, respond to emails over the weekend, or cover for others when the situation requires it. And many jobs are simply not 40-hour-per-week roles. However, some companies and some bosses take advantage of you, expecting you to put in unsustainable hours. One of the worst expressions in modern management is, "Do more with less." Scope is a function of resources and time.
- Your manager expects you to do personal errands or get involved in their personal life when that was not an explicit part of the job.
- Your manager sees you as an obstacle to their objective. Sometimes a senior manager will hire you and put you in a position working for someone they do not trust. In that case your direct line manager is not really your boss and may try to get you pushed out to deal with this situation.
- Someone on your new team thought they deserved the leadership job. This can be a very difficult problem to overcome, and you may find yourself in a situation where you cannot succeed.

- The organization, either by omission or commission, wants you to do things that you consider to be unethical or illegal. The news is full of stories of whistleblowers who have identified behaviors in their organizations they considered to be unethical. While some people simply leave those organizations, others feel an obligation to take a different stand.

Dealing with a toxic manager means dealing with someone who bullies, harasses, verbally abuses, or discriminates against you. A toxic work environment is a workplace where you are unable to do your job ethically and legally because of the behavior of the people around you. Moreover, the behavior should be observable by others, rather than only seen by one individual.

We are using the word *toxic* as it is commonly used to refer to managers and work environments generally. According to Manfred Kets de Vries, a toxic leader usually has either a personality disorder or a mood disorder.[ix] "If the boss's psychological makeup is warped, business plans, ideas, interactions, and even the systems and structure of the organization itself, will reflect his or her pathologies."

For others, it is less about their "mental demons" and more about their verbal and emotional behavior. The words and the tone of the people around you convey hostility, cynicism, and a disregard for the feelings of others. They show disrespect, and typically make you feel disempowered and incompetent. There is usually little doubt about these managers and these environments. Everyone, from the entry-level workers to the C-suite, knows about it.

If you find yourself in this kind of environment, run, do not walk, to the nearest exit door. Even if you love the job itself, you should not tolerate being belittled, verbally abused, or grossly overworked. And, if you are asked to do things that are unethical or illegal, this will only lead to problems for you down the road.

One of the particularly toxic aspects of this kind of work environment is that it undermines your confidence. You may think that you will always be haunted by this boss' negative view of you. While we cannot guarantee that this will not happen, it is our experience that people's fears of the repercussions of leaving toxic environments are significantly overblown.

The only options you should consider other than leaving are talking to a lawyer about filing a lawsuit against the company or exploring the idea of being a whistleblower. Both of these may apply in the case of a toxic organization. The former primarily applies in the case of a toxic manager. The terms "harassment" and "hostile work environment" have specific legal meanings, particularly in the context of the Equal Employment Opportunities Commission. You should speak to an attorney before using these words in the workplace. However, there are legal protections, and you should consider those options if you think your company has violated the law.

Will the Job Bring You Value or Meaning?

Last but not least is the question of motivation. Given what you know about the job, and what you know about the culture of the organization and your manager's expectations, the question is whether you will be gratified by doing the job. We are not asking if this is your ideal job, or if it meets your needs 100% of the time. We all have to do work that we don't enjoy or that does not benefit us. Hopefully it benefits someone else. But if you are not doing work you enjoy or benefit from at least 50% of the time, the fact that you can do the job and can adapt to the environment does not matter. A general and unscientific rule of thumb is that if you feel good about the work and the environment 60% of the time, or more, you are doing great. And less than 50%, and you are probably not in the right job for any length of time.

Observe your emotions   Do you feel depressed or unmotivated every time you go to work?

1. Are you having trouble sleeping or losing your appetite when you think about work?
2. Is the way you feel about work interfering with friendships or family relationships?
3. Are there senior leaders who offer support, guidance, that can make up for the behavior of your manager?

Remind yourself of your strengths, preferences, ideal environment, and long-term objectives   Your strengths are likely (but not always) going to align with what you enjoy—most of us enjoy doing what we do well. Think about what you enjoy doing from a task and then style perspective. Lay out your ideal job criteria, and make sure they line up with your preferences and likes or strengths. Last, stand in your own future and consider what you want it to be like personally and professionally, answering "What matters to me, now? What will matter to me over time?"

The Moment of Truth

It's time to decide. There are four options:

I do want this job. I care and am willing to commit to doing the work the organization needs from me the most, and adapting to the culture, even if my plan is to change it in the long run. If this is your answer, go on to Part 3. There, we'll discuss what changes to make in order to build your influence and increase your impact so that your value shines through to the organization. You are on your way!

I do not want to do the work required in this job, or am not good at the work required for this job, or I do not want to keep working for my current manager, but I like the organization I work for (its values, its mission, its culture). If this is your answer, go to Part 4, Chapter 10. Here, we'll talk about how to position yourself so that you increase the likelihood of finding other options within your organization.

I am not in the right job for me, either because I am not good at it, I don't like the environment, or it doesn't meet my needs. If this is your answer, go to Part 4, Chapter 11. Here, we will help you think through how to start on your search for new opportunities and challenges that align with your needs, strengths, and interests.

I am unsure. There may be benefits and costs to the job, and you are not clear about the balance of them. There are endless ways for people to be unsure, or what psychologists call ambivalent. Ambivalence is a psychological state in which a person has conflicting or mutually exclusive ideas or feelings about a situation or person, and hence cannot make a choice between two or more options.

Ambivalence is a painful place to be. It is a very personal form of being stuck, and usually comes with a fair amount of anxiety, stress, or self-doubt. Be wary of becoming a "chronic contemplator," someone who is stuck between the pros and cons of their situation, and as a result does nothing.[x] Consider the following options:

- Go back to the work you have done, look over the worksheets you completed, and see if there is something you missed. Is there something that you did not write down that might sway you? Or is there something holding you in place that you have not made explicit?

- You may want to put all these materials down for a few weeks and come back to them. People can get so focused on analyzing their situation that they lose track of the experience. Stepping away and coming back can help you clarify your plan, your objectives, and interests, and help you clarify what you feel in the role you are in.

- Talk to a loved one, a friend, or a trusted colleague. Share your thinking with someone who does not have a vested interest in what you do, but simply believes that you deserve to have a job, and a manager, in an organization you enjoy.

- Do a gut test. Make a choice, any choice. Write it down on a piece of paper and go to sleep for the night. When you wake up in the morning, look at your piece of paper and see how you feel. It you feel good, you made the right choice. If you feel stressed or anxious, go back and reconsider your choice.

The bottom line is, being stuck is a lousy place to be and is not helpful for you or others. But be careful. Sometimes, people get so fed up with their ambivalence that they make an impulsive choice, and then find that they cannot revisit it. Often times your ambivalence is due to a fear of failure or "loss of face." Take a look at Chapter 10, where we talk about how to resolve the feelings and behaviors that come with this crisis.

Key Takeaways

Now that you know the truth about what your organization "actually" needs from you, do you still want this job? This is the commit or change moment.

End Notes

[i] Collins, J. C. (2001). *Good to great: Why some companies make the lead—and others don't.* New York: HarperCollins.

[ii] Breaugh, J. A. (2017). The contribution of job analysis to recruitment. *The Wiley Blackwell handbook of the psychology of recruitment, selection and employee retention*, pp. 12–28. Hoboken, NJ: John Wiley & Sons; Vandaveer, V. V., Lowman, R. L., Pearlman, K., & Brannick, J. P. (2016). "A practice analysis of coaching psychology: Toward a foundational competency model." *Consulting Psychology Journal: Practice and Research*, 68(2): 118.

[iii] Ferdman, B. M., Prime, J., & Riggio, R. (2020). *Inclusive leadership: Transforming diverse lives, workplaces, and societies.* NY: Routledge.

[iv] Maurer, R. (December 12, 2018). Why are workers quitting their jobs in record numbers? Society of Human Resources Management (SHRM.org). Retrieved February 7, 2021 from https://www.shrm.org/resourcesandtools/hr-topics/talent-acquisition/pages/workers-are-quitting-jobs-record-numbers.aspx

[v] Reichert, J., & Bognar, S. (2019). American Factory. Netflix.

vi Bourke, J., & Titus, A. (2019). Why Inclusive Leaders Are Good for Organizations, and How to Become One. Harvard Business Review. Retrieved February 7, 2021 from https://hbr.org/2019/03/why-inclusive-leaders-are-good-for-organizations-and-how-to-become-one

vii Bradt, G. (2015). What VW's Next CEO Must Do to Save The Organization. Forbes. Retrieved February 7, 2021 from https://www.forbes.com/sites/george-bradt/2015/09/23/what-vws-next-ceo-must-do-to-save-the-organization/?sh=46c44 0a7d557.

viii Shannon, E. (Sept 23, 2015). How Two Dogged Clean Air Sleuths Exposed Massive VW Deceit. Retrieved from https://www.ewg.org/enviroblog/2015/09/how-two-dogged-clear-air-sleuths-exposed-massive-vw-deceit

ix De Vries, M. F. (2014). Coaching the toxic leader. Harvard Business Review, 92(4): 100.

x DiClemente, C. C., & Velasquez, M. M. (2001). Motivational interviewing and the stages of change. In Miller, W., & Rolnick, S., *Motivational interviewing: Preparing people for change.* (pp. 201–216). NY, NY: Guilford Press.

PART III

Plan A: Grow Your Influence and Impact

CHAPTER 7

Build Your Personal Strategic Plan™

Set Your Course to Increased Influence and Impact

3 First, collect the data	4 Distill the data	5 What if there's bias?	6 Do you still want this job?	7 Make a new plan	8 Work your plan	9 Now, look for more

"Yesterday I was clever, so I wanted to change the world. Today I am wise, so I am changing myself."

—Rumi

At an organizational level, future capability planning is a logical, essential step in a strategic planning process. Once an organization identifies the mission and the strategy it is going to pursue to be successful, it needs to figure out how to bridge the operational and organizational gaps between its aspirational objectives and current reality, as required by that strategy.

For you as an individual, Personal Strategic Planning (PSP) is about thinking through the critical changes to your priorities, tone, and behavior that you discovered to be misaligned in Part 2. You'll start by identifying your mission and values, and then move on to identify your strategic priorities.

Finally, you will create a set of specific plans or initiatives to take on the work needed in the way needed, to increase your influence and impact.

Most people should have a Personal Strategic Plan. It sets the direction for career growth (or personal growth, in some cases). This is not an inflexible structure, however. One should always be flexible, particularly if interesting opportunities come along. But a plan is generally useful in keeping you on track under normal circumstances.

Michael Ignatieff was as academic and author from 1976 to 2006, teaching at august institutions like Cambridge, Oxford, Harvard, and Toronto. His plan was clearly established. In 2006, however, he ran for a seat in the House of Commons, and two years later was elected leader of the Liberal Party in 2009, which he held for two years before returning to academia.

We have provided a template for your Personal Strategic Plan in Worksheet 7.1 at the end of this chapter. Each element builds on what you learned about yourself, your organization, your team, and your manager. This, and the next chapter are about building and leveraging your Personal Strategic Plan to enhance your influence and impact. We recommend you start by modifying the mission you worked on in Chapter 2, to make it applicable to your current work situation. We call this the Working Mission. A working mission defines your mission in the context of your organization's mission.

Then, revisit the values you outlined, and adapt to your current situation. We call these your Ways of Working. They are more specific and directive than your values.

Third, identify the strategies—what we call, in this context, your change objectives—that will help you achieve your mission. In Chapter 8 we will define the tactics or actions that will help you achieve the strategies.

Your Working Mission

In the first part of this book, you worked through the relationship between your mission and values, those of your organization, and the alignment between them. Our intent here is to understand and build a plan that enables you to be your optimal self in the context of your current (and future) role.

Your working mission reflects what you are trying to achieve that will meet your needs as a working person. Remember, you have decided you are in the right job, in the right organization. While your personal working mission has to contribute to your organization's mission, it does not have to be the same. It should explain, at a very high level, what you want to accomplish in your role, and how you want to have impact on the organization.

It should also align with your manager's mission, or what you believe it to be. Again, aligned does not mean that they are the same. What it means is that your working mission will support your manager's working mission. Keep in mind that we did not make this book about discovering and excelling at what your organization (and boss) *want*. It's about discovering and excelling at what they *really need*.[i]

Examples of personal missions vary widely and are unique for different individuals. They include:

"Use my experience and knowledge as a marketer to help both our services and our people leverage their strengths in a way that others immediately understand their value."

"Leverage deep data science and industry expertise to push the company and my team to think differently, challenge the status quo, and improve our competitive position in the marketplace."

"Improve the standardization and automation of the work of the operations group, so that we can respond to our customers faster, more clearly, and more effectively. I also want to improve my team's strengths with technology so that they can continue to have an effect on others."

"Guide, support, and advise others to help them succeed so that our business can thrive."

If you are not clear about your working mission, review Worksheet 2.3 to sort out what the short- and long-term benefits are for what you are doing in your job. Record your working mission in Worksheet 7.1.

Your Ways of Working

Look back at the values you identified in Chapter 2 and remind yourself what is most important to you in terms of personal characteristics, environment, achievement, understanding, and the like. Now, clarify which of your values are most relevant to your job. Ideally these are consistent with your organization or team. These will be your ways of working.

One way to do this is to turn the most relevant values into more specific guidelines for yourself in your role. If, for example, you say you value collaboration, your way of working might be "Build alignment with all key stakeholders before making mission-critical decisions." Another example of ways of working comes from Othmarr Amman.

In the 1920s, renowned engineer Othmarr Ammann was not surprised The Port Authority rejected his proposal to increase the strength of the George Washington Bridge's pillars to support an extra level of traffic if needed later. The Port Authority had chosen his design because it cost less than other proposals.

Ammann completed construction of the bridge in 1931, six months ahead of schedule and under budget, making his clients very happy.

Decades later, the authorities came back to Ammann asking how much it would cost to strengthen the pillars to support the extra level of traffic that was now needed. His answer?

Nothing.

Ammann knew the bridge would need to be expanded. He also knew he could save his clients significant money over time if he added the strengthened supports despite their having rejected his proposal. And he still delivered everything the clients requested ahead of schedule and under budget.

Othmarr's value was either customer service, exceeding expectations, or something similar. His way of working was, "Do what the customer needs, not only what they want today."

Self-Awareness and Self-Regulation

Guest Contributor: Hy Pomerance, Ph.D.

Eric was managing director of a global financial services firm. He was legal counsel for the bank's wealth management division. A highly intelligent man in his late thirties, he was rapidly advancing through the organization. Known for his quick problem-solving skills and extraordinary communication skills, he also had a reputation for intellectually intimidating his colleagues.

His boss, the global general counsel, was concerned that his behavior and attitude was getting in the way of his continued growth and impeding the rest of his team's work, who were afraid to express their views. I was brought in to help Eric improve his relationships with his peers and develop his team.

The work began with a traditional 360° feedback process. Hearing about his negative impact from different perspectives and experiences was essential to grab Eric's attention and help him to "see" blind spots. It was difficult for Eric to accept the feedback. He heard how scary, dismissive, often interrupting and strident, his views could be. His team experienced him as not listening, having a strong need to be right, and only recognizing the work of a select few on the team, mostly men. He acknowledged the comments, from both his boss and members of the team, and began to recognize he had to improve if he was to continue to advance at the bank. Most importantly, he saw how his need to demonstrate his intellectual prowess was destroying trust with his colleagues. This was the key to developing motivation to change—he realized that his current behavior was counter-productive to what the bank needed from him.

This realization was also critical to his growing awareness of the core mission of his job: Scale his brilliant legal mind and problem-solving skill to empower his team. We developed a practical plan focused on areas for change. Our approach created a safe space where Eric would practice with feedback from a trusted colleague.

He started with managing his need to be right and not listening. He practiced pausing while others finished their points. He avoided interrupting so that he could understand what others were saying. We began with one colleague: Eric patiently listened to what she was trying to do and why. He then asked his team to let him know if he interrupted. He gave others permission to remind him if he "slipped" and interrupted. Ultimately, he knew that giving full attention and listening would show respect and build trust, which was his underlying goal. Eric then focused on acknowledging others. He began seeing the valuable contributions by the team and put aside his embarrassment about praising them for their ideas. Resisting the temptation to one-up them became easier. He found ways to support the team's work. Eric's goal was not to show his team how smart he was (I reminded him that he knew that) but to encourage the team to use their smarts and to build their trust. His issue-spotting skill had caused others to feel self-doubt and was intimidating.

One technique we used was to take notes after meetings, reflecting on how he felt and what he noticed in others' behavior. Our goal here was to help him recognize what he was feeling about his behavior. This work continued for three months and was then followed up with a short pulse survey of his team and peers. This time the feedback was that Eric was no longer belittling his team with his intellect. They felt he valued their contributions more, seemed more relaxed, and even showed a sense of humor they had never seen before.

The key to his understanding what his boss needed from him was unlocking the potential of his talented team so that he could scale his problem-solving skill. He realized the mission was not "doing the work himself" but rather leading the team to do the work. Through increased self-awareness and self-regulation, Eric became aligned with what the organization needed from him.

Your Change Objectives

Your change objectives are the behaviors, attitudes, and relationships you want to improve, adapt, or leverage that will help you achieve your mission. We suggest limiting your focus to three, because trying to change more than three things at a time, even if one is a strength to begin with, will diffuse your efforts, and make it hard to know what, if anything, has made the difference in your performance. Consider the following questions as you weigh your objectives:

- How will you shift your priorities to better deliver on the most important parts of your job?
- How will you change your behaviors and attitudes to align with the essential elements of your team's culture, or the organizational culture?
- How will you change your attitude and interactions with your managers, peers, and stakeholders to create and strengthen the relationships necessary to achieve your mission?

You do not need to answer all of these questions, and you may address issues that are not captured by these. The important point is to identify the limited set of changes that will best help you enhance your influence and impact.

Your objectives do not need to be highly detailed or quantitative at this point. These are aspirational statements that you can work on over time by focusing on a wide range of specific actions. The specific "SMART" actions will come in Chapter 8.

There are three major types of change strategy: business-focused, interpersonal, and organizational.

Business-Focused Change Strategies

Many executives are overwhelmed—by emails, by meetings, by initiatives, or other tactical burdens. They describe not having control over their schedule or feeling like the demands of the business are running them. Others feel as if they are stuck in the movie, Groundhog Day, addressing the same problems over and over. In the majority of cases, this is not a problem of time management, but rather priority management: How they manage their business.

Leaders who feel time-constrained often suffer from one of three types of priority management challenges:

- They have not clearly established business and personal priorities, so that the urgency of an issue overwhelms its importance.[ii]
- They have not properly structured their team or their business, and have not hired the right people that would allow them to allocate their time to Main Team (direct reports) versus First Team (manager's team members) priorities, and internal and external needs.
- They have not established their operational cadence so that delegation, empowerment, and decision rights are difficult to implement successfully.

Whether you are starting a new role or trying to enhance your influence and impact in an established role, it is essential to get these three domains right, many times before working on any interpersonal or political changes. The reason is simple: Effective leaders and managers have to create the context for others to succeed. You have to ensure that you have the right people, in the right roles, focused on the right things, in the most effective manner. If these elements are not properly set up, *how* you lead and who you align with will not make up for doing the wrong things with the wrong people or in the wrong roles. You may have known a leader who tried to use their evenings and weekends to make up for lack of clarity or resources. This rarely works in the long run.

> *Eleanor was the chief development officer of a large not-for-profit organization. She was successful in meeting her financial goals, but her manager felt she was too deep into the weeds of her people's work. She needed to consider longer-term fundraising as well as ensuring that her team was handling the details right. When we first met, she had 16 people on her team, 12 of whom reported directly to her. It became clear that the number of people and development challenges was overwhelming, making it impossible for her to focus on anything but day-to-day work.*
>
> *We helped her restructure her organization so that she had three major teams, plus two individual contributors who focused on specific donor groups. All of the remaining team members reported to the three team leaders, two focused on high-priority development segments and one on operational processes. Within weeks, Eleanor was able to begin work on longer-term strategic issues, including novel fundraising vehicles and contingency plans.*

We often hear from bosses that one of their high-potential team members needs to "be more strategic," "think big-picture," or "get out of the weeds." Often, this means that the person needs to focus on more important and unresolved business issues. There are a variety of ways to develop these strategic skills, but they all require the scarcest resource in business: Time. People cannot think strategically, or look for unintended consequences in 15-minute increments. They always require the time to read, listen, observe, and think. Again, this becomes a problem of priority management, not thinking *per se*.

Interpersonal Change Strategies

Once you are confident that you have the right strategy, the right people, and the right operational cadence, the next domain is interpersonal change. How you interact with, relate to, and communicate with others is essential to effective influencing. Understanding the interpersonal dynamics and cultural norms of the various groups in your organization is essential to enhancing your influence. Having effective social skills, and relating to others in an authentic, engaging way are equally valuable. Terms like charm, authenticity, respect, listening, and the like are common areas to work on. Many of the skills needed to build your interpersonal influence fall into the broad category of Emotional Intelligence (EQ), in the way that Daniel Goleman and colleagues have defined it.[iii]

The four principal themes of EQ are self-understanding, other-understanding, self-management, and other-management. The first two address how you experience, share, and control your own emotional states. The latter two focus on how you perceive, understand, manage, and prioritize others' emotional states (your ability to use empathy). Although emotions are different from culture, the organizational culture elicits different emotions in different people, and people's emotions are handled differently in each organization's culture.

Empathy is essential to effective interpersonal influence. Empathy enables you to understand another person's perspective without having personally experienced it. Paradoxically, empathy cannot occur without understanding one's own emotional state. That is why some of the work needed to build influence and impact involves learning about your own and others' emotional experiences. Many of our clients do not focus on their own emotions, thinking that one should suppress emotions in the workplace. Understanding your emotions does not mean expressing them, however. Successful executives and managers need to use their own emotional experience, so that they can influence how others feel and act.

Many of the interpersonal areas for growth are not large-scale actions or big personal shifts. Rather, they are small, day-to-day behaviors that convey a lot of information because they occur so frequently. A common example is the manager who walks down the hall, focused on their next meeting or their smartphone. They often do not notice the people they pass, because they are absorbed in their own thoughts. Many people experience this manager as haughty or dismissive, and conclude (often wrongly) that the person does not care about them.

Listening is another common tool for interpersonal influence. Many times, we are so focused on our own concerns that we barely hear what the other person says. Or we disagree, and immediately start thinking about our response instead of listening to the other person. This also unintentionally conveys disrespect, and limits our ability to have a positive influence and impact on others.

People often think of being inspirational as a key element to interpersonal influence. It is important, but there are many ways to be inspirational, ranging from powerful public speaking to simply living by your values every day.

When you are developing interpersonal change strategies, be sure to involve both large-scale behaviors and small actions and responses.

Organizational Change Strategies

"I hate playing politics. People who play political games usually do it because they are 'empty suits' who don't know what to do."

A countless number of people have said some version of this to us over our careers. Most people equate organizational politics with backbiting, zero-sum competitions, and Machiavellian tactics. Some people definitely play these types of games, and we find those manipulations as distasteful as our clients do.

To accomplish work efficiently in an organization, you have to have political intelligence (PQ). PQ, a cousin to IQ and EQ, refers to the intersection of interpersonal relationships and organizational needs that enables work to move faster and smoother in a complex system. When done well, organizational politics involves the development and maintenance of a network of colleagues at all levels of the organization. Colleagues will work with you because it is expected, but they will happily help and support you in achieving your objectives if you have a strong, mutual relationship with them. As one executive explained to his very challenging business development lead, "You have to earn the right to tell people what to do who don't report to you. You do that by building a relationship with them."

PQ also involves knowing how decisions are made in an organization, and who has influence with whom. We have found that most executives build close, trusted relationships with a few others, and rely on them for information and insights. Ensuring you have a good relationship with some of those influencers can make it easier to communicate your ideas and acquire the scarce resources you need to deliver what is expected.

Finally, PQ helps you stand up for, and advocate on behalf of, your team members. Many people do not like promoting their work, and in some cultures self-advocacy is perceived as arrogant or "unseemly." At the same time, it is the job of a leader to recognize their team members and help them stand out as valued contributors in their own right. Knowing where to do this, and how to do it is an essential part of having influence in organizations large and small.

Once you have established what you want to change to enhance your influence and impact, you need to shift to execution mode. This means taking the steps you need on a regular basis to make the changes you have identified. In the next chapter we will describe how to translate these objectives into specific actions.

Didi's team of account managers consistently exceeded their goals, but she was frustrated by both her manager and the company she worked for. She felt she had been passed over for a promotion and was shown neither the respect nor the recognition for several significant accomplishments over the past two years. She was considering looking for another job but agreed to work with an executive coach.

Based on a 360° assessment and several personality tests, Bill and Didi agreed that her success at driving results and her ability to keep her team focused and motivated were significant strengths. These were coming, however, at the cost of her effectiveness with peers and internal customers. Although she was seen as a driver, the unintended effect of her drive was that others felt she was focused on her own agenda rather than reaching shared solutions with her stakeholders. In addition, she prioritized the work itself, without taking the time to build relationships that would make others want to collaborate with her. Efforts to manage the team's workflow were seen by some of her internal customers as resistant or unresponsive to them.

Based on these observations, Didi and Bill agreed that she would work with her new manager and her key stakeholders to revisit their business objectives, and make sure they were all aligned with what was needed. Her objectives for the coaching work drew directly from this:

1. *Develop a clear understanding of what all of her stakeholders wanted and needed from her team, including her manager and her top internal customers. (A business focused change)*

2. *Look for win-win solutions rather than "setting limits" on what seemed at first to be unreasonable requests. (A political change)*

3. *Shift her approach to communication—both formal and informal—to demonstrate the benefits to her customers and stakeholders rather than the quality of the work they did. (An interpersonal change)*

Didi focused on these three change priorities and continued to produce the results she had always delivered. By the end of the year, she received both the promotion she was looking for and a significant increase in pay. More importantly, her manager and her manager's manager both told her that she was much more effective, and she received excellent feedback from her stakeholders.

Personal Strategic Plan™

Download an editable worksheet at **www.BermanLeadership.com/ InfluenceandImpact**

Worksheet 7.1   **Personal Strategic Plan™**

Working Mission:			
Ways of Working (Values/Guidelines):			
	Change Strategies *(Identify as Business-focused, Interpersonal, Organizational-focused)*		
Focus/Strategy	Tactics/Actions	Success	Target Date
Focus Area 1			
Focus Area 2			
Focus Area 3			

Key Takeaways

Document your Personal Strategic Plan. This should include your mission adjusted for the context of your organization now (Working Mission); your values as they apply to the current situation (Ways of Working); your priorities for change, which may include business, interpersonal and organization-focused strategies (Change Strategies) and the tactics and actions associated with them.

End Notes

[i] Bradt, G. (2013, November 26). Why You Don't Get to Choose Your Mission. It Chooses You. Forbes. Retrieved February 7, 2021 from https://www.forbes.com/sites/georgebradt/2013/11/26/why-you-dont-get-to-choose-your-mission-it-chooses-you/?sh=3016a43a221b

[ii] For those not familiar with the Eisenhower Matrix, described by Stephen Covey, here is the reference: Covey, S. (2013). *The 7 habits of highly effective people.* New York: Simon and Schuster.

[iii] Goleman, D., Boyatzis, R. E., & McKee, A. (2017). *Primal leadership unleashing the power of emotional intelligence.* Cambridge: Harvard Business Review Press.; Boyatzis, R. E., Goleman, D., & Rhee, K. (2000). Clustering competence in emotional intelligence: Insights from the emotional competence inventory (ECI). *Handbook of Emotional Intelligence*, 99(6): 343–362.

CHAPTER 8

Work Your Growth Plan, Build Your Influence

Putting Your Plan into Action

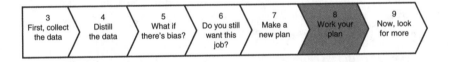

| 3 First, collect the data | 4 Distill the data | 5 What if there's bias? | 6 Do you still want this job? | 7 Make a new plan | 8 Work your plan | 9 Now, look for more |

"We choose to do this not because it is easy, but because it is hard, because the challenge is one that we are willing to accept, one we are unwilling to postpone, and one which we intend to win."

—John F. Kennedy

Growth Plans Are All About the Details

Having an outsized impact often appears to come from big bold moves that happen from time to time. Once you have nailed a game-winning objective, people look to you to do it again. You have earned a reputation as a breakthrough player. Like most breakthroughs, however, they are invariably built on the small actions you took multiple times a day for weeks or months that added up to the person you are and what you stand for.

Similarly, enhancing your ability to influence and impact others in your workplace involves setting stretch objectives followed by a series of small steps, executed on a regular basis over time. We identified the large objectives in Chapter 7. In this chapter, we address the detailed planning, consistent execution, and adaptation to external circumstances needed to have the influence and impact you are striving for.

A well-crafted plan is an essential start, and requires persistence and commitment. In turn, persistence is invaluable until the situation changes or you encounter unplanned obstacles. At that point, you need to exchange persistence for agility, until you have dealt with the challenge, of course. Then you have to go back to being persistent.

Think of your growth plan as continuous quality improvement (CQI) rather than a "one and done" project, relying on a growth mindset.[i] By adopting the Plan, Do, Evaluate, Adjust approach[ii] of CQI, your actions are testing a hypothesis.[iii] The results will provide you with useful information even if the result is not exactly what you expected. You can change the plan to adapt to new information, while maintaining the same overall objective.

Bill's experience with changing his own behavior is a good example.

Ten years ago, I was diagnosed with a herniated lumbar disk in my spine. The pain became worse over a period of months, and interfered with most aspects of life. What was worse, I had disc surgery decades earlier, and re-ruptured the same disk ten years after that. I was quite worried about repeating that procedure.

I worked with two chiropractors, a physical therapist, an acupuncturist, and a massage therapist. Nothing helped. I finally consulted a spine surgeon, who told me I had a 50% likelihood of success. Feeling desperate, I agreed to try one more physical therapist on a friend's recommendation.

Toward the end of the evaluation session, he stopped and said, "How much time are you willing to commit to feeling better?" When I demurred, he really pushed me. He insisted on a specific time commitment for a specific number of days per week before he would work with me. I committed to 20 minutes, 4x/week, which was 79 minutes more than I had been doing. He agreed and said, "If you stick with that consistently, I will be able to help you improve your quality of life and avoid surgery."

Within three months I was moving and active. He continued to give me additional challenges, increasing my time commitment when I could, and increasing the intensity of my workouts when I had less time. Making that commitment of time to him made all the difference compared to everyone else I had seen.

Set Smart Actions for Each Objective

A fundamental tenet of learning theory[iv] is that positive feedback increases the likelihood that you will repeat that behavior. And until you start getting feedback from others, the best way to reward yourself is to set small, incremental SMART[v] goals (Specific, Measurable, Achievable, Relevant, Time Bound).

Actions are best if they involve multiple steps along the path. The number of steps can vary, although our experience says you should have at least three, and usually five to seven steps to achieve the goal. There are a number of sources for specific actions for growth plans, but you can probably identify unique ones that will be most helpful to you in your context.[vi]

Involve Others

Your first decision is how you want to roll out your growth plan. You have two options, with infinite variations in between. You can choose to work your change plan quietly, making behavioral and attitude shifts with no fanfare, and let people discover them on their own. Or, you can be more open and explicit about the shift, declaring your intentions to your peers, your team, and senior management.

Each approach has benefits and costs. For the former, your privacy allows you to change your approach without anyone noticing and saves you from embarrassment if you are unable to make the changes for some reason. However, people take a long time to notice changes, particularly with people they have known for a long time. So, it may take months for people to become aware of your changes.

For the latter, you typically can get support and encouragement from colleagues, and research has shown that external commitment increases your adherence to the plan.[vii] If you are not committed to the change, you risk falling back to old habits, which undermines others' confidence in future successes. In general, we recommend you involve someone else in your effort to change. As Peter Drucker said, "Unless commitment is made, there are only promises and hopes; but no plans."

Engage Your Manager in Your Process

At a minimum, involve your boss. Most of the time it is in their interest for you to succeed and, therefore, in your best interest to seek your manager's input and support. Review your plan with them on a regular basis; highlight what you have accomplished; explicitly ask for their insights; and point them in the right direction to best leverage their strengths and resources.

Alignment Is Everything

Guest Contributor: Joe Garbus

Alignment is everything and all things, when it comes to optimizing your success in your role. As a close colleague explained to me, "The test for true alignment is unsupervised action." When every one of your stakeholders contributes by acting in alignment with that role, you optimize the role. Consequently, the devil is in the details and those closest to the work, on the ground, can make or break the success of a role.

This past year, I had the privilege to work with William, a long-tenured regional executive who was tapped to run a large, complex global function. As an internal talent leader, I support many executives as they onboard to new roles. We spend a lot of time on vision, mission, strategy, team cohesion, key initiatives, short-term wins, and the ever-present, "Make sure your boss's ideas are in the plan." I encourage them to use "kitchen English" to convey the strategy on one page. We also clarify the obstacles with clear mitigation plans.

William's new business had stabilized over the previous few years but was far from achieving its revenue potential and value to clients externally and colleagues internally. The organization still lacked a cohesive strategy, and was highly matrixed globally. Many colleagues at the ground level in various countries contributed to the function off the side of their desks rather than in a full-time capacity.

In William's case, he was working effectively to incorporate the views of two bosses as well as get the CEO excited about the vision. We also made sure that he aligned a whole variety of stakeholders at the regional level. This was particularly important with those who would nominally agree with the strategy but exert full control over resources and priorities for their teams. For instance, were colleagues spending too much time administering a process to do what is required versus finding ways to add to the client experience and local understanding of the strategic needs of the client? It took a concerted effort for William to understand the real choices that local leaders needed to make. He needed to frame the strategy in language that described gains and losses. He also had to convince them that the gain was more advantageous than the loss: strategically, operationally, and even politically. The key to achieving alignment was balancing an inspiring vision for change with the reality of hard work needed to deliver it.

All too often, we shy away from the conversations that test for true alignment. Mapping out wins and losses for key stakeholders is not just a change management technique. It is critical to determining how best to execute, how to authentically communicate, and how to understand the consequences of decisions to be made. In fact, changing messaging and keeping it fresh takes on additional importance. Ultimately, success in role depends on all the variety of choices stakeholders are making when those in the role are not around.

Start by bringing your manager up to speed. Remember they have most recently been thinking about something other than what you're working on. Give them the general context: "I am working on my own professional development, and I want your input on what I am thinking of doing." Share your plan and focus on the headlines of your efforts to date. Spare them the details of what you have done, focusing on the results rather than the process, unless they specifically ask. How you have made progress is usually less important than what you are thinking of doing next.

Context Focus here on your objectives and the rationale for why that is important to them, to you, and to key stakeholders. Ask your manager to confirm your assumptions and improve on them. When you approach them with an open, growth-oriented mindset, they will feel much more comfortable helping you than if they have to start by telling you what you need to work on.

Approach There are many ways to refocus your work and your interactions, as described in Chapter 7. Lay out your actions with an eye toward spending more time on the areas that are most relevant to your impact and influence, and how this will benefit your manager as well. Your ask here is for your boss to challenge the options you considered and help you improve your choices.

Colleagues Make sure your manager understands which colleagues you have brought in to help you with your thinking or implementation so far. Ask them to point you in the direction of other people with whom you should connect.

Leverage their clout Put your manager to work. They can be most effective when focused on their own strengths: For managers, that includes finding resources, facilitating connections, and removing obstacles. Your boss, or their boss, will likely have access to different resources than you do.

If you need other human, technical, operational, or financial resources to accomplish your objectives, and can't secure them on your own, ask your boss to reallocate them. Reallocating resources is a core part of your boss' job. They can best support your strategy by identifying and allocating resources to the right place in the right way at the right time over time. Or, if they do not have access, ask your boss to connect you with people who can.

Implement Your Changes: The Three Parts of Behavior Change

There are three aspects to making changes in your influence and impact:

1. The first is making the changes that you have identified as important to you, your manager, and your organization.
2. The second is getting other people to notice that you have made a change.
3. The third is getting others to believe that the changes are real rather than cosmetic.

Making the Change

We use a version of Roger Neill's "Best Current Thinking" approach for problem-solving. It's a powerful tool that focuses attention on possible solutions rather than a single recommended solution:[viii]

- Share your going-in perspective on the problem, context, and best current thinking around potential options.

- Answer their questions for clarification and encourage them to highlight what they think works best in your current thinking and barriers to making it work even better.

- Work together to find ways to overcome the barriers to make the best current thinking even better.

- Take back ownership either to get input from others, implement the plan, or both, continuing to improve as you go.

Insight

Remarkably, we all believe we can make significant changes in our own approach but are deeply skeptical that others can "change their spots." There are a great many more expressions regarding people's difficulty with change than there are about the ease of change, for good reason. On the other hand, many people exaggerate the degree to which they can motivate others to change because they want them to. People are capable of change, when there is sufficient intrinsic or extrinsic motivation for it.

Hypothesize   You have set your objectives and identified specific actions you are going to take to achieve the goal. You have (hopefully) shared those plans with your manager. You might also review with your team and with others to check your thinking. If they can improve your growth plan, so much the better.

Note there are times when you do not want others' input at this point. This might be when your hypothesis is especially personal. In cases like this, they'll see the result of your changes and the impact on them and the organization. They don't need to know what triggered it. As Voltaire said, "There are truths which are not for all men, nor for all times."

Act   Your SMART goals and actions are not carved in stone, but rather are theories that you are going to test. Some of the actions you take may work beautifully, while others do not move you toward the goal. Do not give up on them immediately but take the approach that these are hypotheses that can be used or discarded based on the evidence. Be sure to set timelines for each action. Having a completion date helps you to persist long enough to evaluate its effectiveness, and prevents you from getting distracted from the objective.

Evaluate   Each of your hypotheses needs to be tested and validated. They could be 100% right, partly right, or wholly wrong—your task is to figure that out. For each hypothesis, what outcome do you expect to see? Do not base your conclusions on a single observation. Test your SMART goals and actions for a few weeks before analyzing your "data." You should have several experiences with the change before making any decisions.

Your hypotheses should tell you not only what to do but what you expect to happen. Test your actions by tracking the impact on your team, your manager, your stakeholders. Are you seeing a change in how they respond to you? Are you feeling a change internally? How do these changes align with what you were expecting? Remember that your experience will probably include anxiety, trepidation, or concern, as this is a potentially new experience. Differentiate anxiety caused by situations you have been avoiding (changing your old behavior) from threats that you want to avoid.

Be careful of confounding your tests. Test one or two hypotheses at any given time so you can see the impact of that change. If you test more than a couple at one time, you can't figure out which one made the impact. To reinforce the point, we started this conversation by noting that many people are unintentionally focused on the wrong parts of their job. Make sure your change is making an impact on what your manager and the organization really needs, rather than what feels good to you.

If the impact is not what you'd hoped for, planned for, or expected, there are a couple of reasons why that could be the case. 1) You might not have done exactly what you'd planned. 2) Others might not have done exactly what you'd hoped, planned, or expected them to do. 3) Your plan didn't work.

Revise   Based on your observations of the effect of your change, make revisions to your SMART goals and actions. Once you have collected your data and tested your hypotheses, you may have to make some revisions. In fact, we've never known anyone to get these hypotheses right at the first try. There are always nuances that need to be tweaked. Do not be afraid to make modifications; you will only get better with an iterative process of hypothesize, implement, evaluate, and revise.

Getting Others to Notice

You will be aware of your own change quickly. You will feel different, and you may observe that others respond to you differently. Despite your awareness, few others will see the change—even your manager, who is aware of your efforts, may not notice anything different. Sometimes letting people know you are working to change helps with this, but often your shifts still go unnoticed for weeks, even months. You have to do the right things, consistently, over substantial periods of time, to turn things around. If you have been doing the wrong job for a while, it will take some time for your manager to notice that you are doing anything different.

Change-ability

Guest Contributor: Aithan Shapira, MFA Ph.D.

The profound uncertainty of our time has redefined the literacy of success—it now requires that you have the stability to change, and the change-ability to remain stable. Change-ability is increasing the range of choices available to you and the ability to move fluidly between them in order to meet the demands of the moment in evolving contexts. The challenge with change-ability is: Why would I change, if everything I've done until now is what got me here? The practice: Engage with the recoiling part of yourself that doesn't want to change.

I never understood goalies. When an object is hurtling toward me at 60 mph my human instinct is to duck, not to throw my body in front of it. High-performing goalies are continually training at transmuting that fear into purpose-driven action at this moment of opportunity.

Similarly, uncertainty creates profound anxiety for many of us. It is creativity that allows us to harness the opportunity of the unknown. Much like an artist, the distress of a blank slate is a high-potential moment—fertile for innovation, change, and growth. The art of change-ability is the practice of knowing how to be when you don't know what to do.

Why? Human nature. Have you ever changed your hairstyle or color, shaved a beard or mustache, or changed your wardrobe, and no one seems to notice? It usually takes a while, and people will say, "Did you change something? You look different, but I can't quite tell what." We establish mental models of the people in our lives, and we tend to see those models when we look at them, rather than seeing them as they are.

Persistence counts. The only way to break through those mental models is repeated evidence to the contrary, that you help people be aware of. There are tricks to maintaining consistency during this time. Use a checklist to make sure you are doing the things that are in your plan consistently. Set alerts on your smartphone. Put reminders on your screen savers. Concrete symbols of the change needed can be extremely helpful.

> *In order to remind a newly minted CEO that his words had a much greater impact than when he was a senior vice president, Bill bought him a megaphone to keep on his desk as a symbol of the increased impact of his voice on others simply because of his title. Every time he started to raise his voice, he would see the megaphone and remember to control his speech.*

In some cases, you can even bring attention to it explicitly. For example, tell team members, "I'm making some changes in how I handle these business meetings, can you let me know if you notice a difference?" Or enlist trusted colleagues in your efforts: "If you notice me getting frustrated, give me a signal so I can sit back and calm myself before speaking."

At the end of each week, write down what you have done differently, and if you have noticed any changes in behavior of the people you work with. Sometimes other people respond to us differently once we make a change, even before they notice a difference consciously. Make a note of how people are responding to you, and how that makes you feel. Give yourself some rewards for making the behavior changes, even when others have not yet noticed them. At the same time, challenge yourself. If others are not noticing a change, it may be because you are giving yourself more credit than you should. Sometimes we make a small change, and think it is sufficient, but others are really looking for a bigger change. Make sure you are pushing yourself to do as much as you possibly can.

Getting Others to Believe

But noticing is not enough. You need them to believe the change is real. Of course, this only works if the change is actually real, if you persist in the change and embed it into your own habits and practices. You are likely to fall back to old behaviors from time to time despite your best efforts. Few people shift their focus or their approach and stay with the change 100%.

Insight

Do not be tempted to find new behaviors or attitudes to change. Stay focused on the critical few things in your development plan. As the change of behavior becomes more comfortable and familiar, people have a tendency to start to pay less attention to it, feeling, "I have this down." These are the times when you are most likely to revert to old behaviors. Slips are minor to you, but they are a sign to others that you were just "putting on good face." Stick with it and be wary of feeling cocky.

Unfortunately, these slips set you back, especially if you are changing a negative behavior. The negativity bias is a well-documented phenomenon. Or one of several other biases may have come into play as well:[ix]

1. **Negativity** bias: Negative experiences are remembered more and lead you to believe negative experiences to a greater degree than positive experiences. People believe in negative behavior much more strongly than positive behavior.[x]

2. **Frequency** bias: When you hear or see the same behavior repeated intermittently over time, you will be more inclined to believe it.

3. **Recency** bias: When making a decision, something you learned or observed recently will carry more weight than information you learned previously.

4. **Attachment** bias: People easily avoid making a change because they do not want to disrupt the status quo, or hold on to what they already have.

5. **Escalation** bias: When you start down a path, you look for evidence to support your direction and at your peril choose to ignore warning signs.

Anticipate and proactively hold yourself accountable for setbacks. Own up to them with the people they affect and get back on track. Do not let them derail you. Remember, changing behaviors and attitudes is difficult and takes time.

Key Takeaways

Successful change requires persistence. The key to a successful change strategy is to work your plan on a regular basis. You can change the tactics while staying true to the strategy. Involve your manager to support your development and gauge your progress. And improve after each iteration.

End Notes

[i] Kaul, A. (2019). "Culture vs strategy: which to precede, which to align?", *Journal of Strategy and Management*, 12(1): 116–136.; Mosanya, M. (2019). "Exploring cultural intelligence relationships with growth mindset, grit, coping and academic stress in the United Arab Emirates." *Middle East Journal of Positive Psychology*, 5(1): 42–59.; Mosanya, M. (2020). "Buffering academic stress during the COVID-19 pandemic related social isolation: Grit and growth mindset as protective factors against the impact of loneliness." *International Journal of Applied Positive Psychology*, 1–16.; Han, S. J., & Stieha, V. (2020). "Growth mindset for human resource development: A scoping review of the literature with recommended interventions." *Human Resource Development Review*, 19(3): 309–331.

[ii] Dennis, P. (2006). *Getting the right things done*. Boston: Lean Enterprise Institute.

[iii] Kegan, R., & Lahey, L. L. (2009b). *Immunity to change: How to overcome it and unlock the potential in yourself and your organization (leadership for the common good)* (1st ed.). Harvard Business Review Press.

[iv] Thurlings, M., Vermeulen, M., Bastiaens, T., & Stijnen, S. (2013). "Understanding feedback: A learning theory perspective." *Educational Research Review*, 9: 1–15.; Gong, Y., Wang, M., Huang, J. C., & Cheung, S. Y. (2017). "Toward a goal orientation-based feedback-seeking typology: Implications for employee performance outcomes." *Journal of Management*, 43(4): 1234–1260.

[v] Doran, G. T. (1981). "There's a S.M.A.R.T. way to write management's goals and objectives." *Management Review*. 70(11): 35–36.; Lawler, J., & Bilson, A. (2009). *Social work management and leadership: Managing complexity with creativity*. New York: Routledge.

[vi] Velsor, V. E., McCauley, C. D., & Ruderman, M. N. (2010). *The Center for Creative Leadership Handbook of Leadership Development* (3rd ed.). San Francisco: Jossey-Bass.; Gebelein, S. H., Nelson-Neuhaus, K. J., Skube, C. J., Lee, D. G., Stevens, L. A., Hellervik, L. W., Davis, B. L., & Marasco, L. (2010). *Successful manager's handbook* (7th ed.). Minneapolis, MN: Personnel Decisions International; Gebelein, S. H., Lee, D. G., Nelson-Heuhaus, K., J., & Sloan, E. B. (1999). *Successful executive's handbook* (2nd ed.). Minneapolis, MN: Personnel Decisions International.

[vii] Epton, T., Currie, S., & Armitage, C. J. (2017). "Unique effects of setting goals on behavior change: Systematic review and meta-analysis." *Journal of Consulting and Clinical Psychology*, 85(12): 1182–1198; Ferdeli, Z., Husein, W., & Hakim, L. (2020). "Effect of employee empowerment and integrity on company performance through organizational commitments as a mediation variables on pt. TGI company." *IAR Journal of Humanities and Social Science*, 1(3).; Vosse, B. J. F., & Aliyu, O. A. (2018). "Determinants of employee trust during organisational change in higher institutions." *Journal of Organizational Change Management*, 31: 1105–1118.

[viii] Bradt, G. (11/27/2018). The Secret Sauce in a Best Current Thinking Approach to Problem Solving. Retrieved from https://www.forbes.com/sites/georgebradt/2018/11/27/the-secret-sauce-in-a-best-current-thinking-approach-to-problem-solving/?sh=50ebdda56b34

[ix] Cohen, G. R. (2009). *Just Ask Leadership: Why Great Managers Always Ask the Right Questions.* New York: McGraw-Hill.

[x] Taylor, Shelley E. (1991). "Asymmetrical effects of positive and negative events: The mobilization-minimization hypothesis" (PDF). *Psychological Bulletin*, 110 (1): 67–85. doi:10.1037/0033-2909.110.1.67.

CHAPTER 9

Take on More Responsibility, Expand Your Impact, and Enjoy the Benefits

Sell Your Value Without Selling Yourself

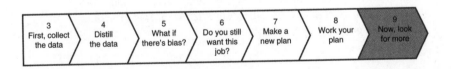

| 3 First, collect the data | 4 Distill the data | 5 What if there's bias? | 6 Do you still want this job? | 7 Make a new plan | 8 Work your plan | 9 Now, look for more |

"Action may not always bring happiness, but there is no happiness without action."

—William James

B y now, you're working your plan and delivering what the organization needs. You've earned the right to have even more influence and impact within your current job. (We will deal with other jobs in the same company in the next chapter.) This is a great place to be. Enjoy it. This is your opportunity to demonstrate what more you can do. And it's a chance to challenge yourself and grow, whether it is developing new capabilities in role, or seeking a promotion.

You do not have to sell yourself. In fact, most leaders we have spoken with find self-promoters to be grating. You do, however have to make it clear that you can and will take on new and bigger responsibilities. Your boss and the organizational leadership cannot know what you want until you show them or tell them about your interests and objectives. Without some type of explicit information, they may assume you are comfortable with your current remit.

New responsibilities will not come automatically. You have to let your leadership know you can and want to do more, either through your actions or words.[i] The more senior you are, the more important it is to let people know that you can handle more, and be clear about what you want to do.

> *Annalise had been the head of marketing for a regional division of the business and had been on a fast track for career growth. She quietly informed her manager that she was adopting a child and was not going to look for continued growth opportunities until her child reached school age—about five years.*
>
> *As a result, he took Annalise off the succession chart, and let her continue in her current role, which she easily managed within a standard schedule.*
>
> *When her daughter reached school age, she came back to her manager (who had now moved to a senior vice president role) and told him she was ready and willing to "get back on the career track."*
>
> *He appreciated her honesty and helped her get a role in another region that was a significant stretch challenge. As expected, she continued to excel and helped drive significant market growth and brand recognition.*

Demonstrate Your Value

How do you let your organization know what you are capable of, and what you are looking for? There are several ways to demonstrate your value to your manager and to your larger organization. You may choose to do one of these, some of these, or all of these. Each element has its benefit, and combined they demonstrate your skills, your leadership, and your willingness to take on additional responsibilities.

Deliver Results, Consistently

It comes as no surprise that consistent delivery of the really important parts of your job, done in a way that matters to the organization, is the *sine qua non* of increasing your influence and impact.

This is particularly valuable when there are headwinds that you manage to push through. Business leaders know that achieving results when the market or the competition presents challenges is much more valuable than when there is smooth sailing. Keep a relentless focus on achieving and exceeding expectations. As one client phrased it,

> *"You have to drive for the vision, adapting but not getting off course. . . . I assessed the situation, laid out the strategy and the roadmap, and had a maniacal focus on executing on the roadmap, always tying it back to the strategy. Don't get distracted by other initiatives."*

There are times where you will miss some of your goals; it is hard to perform perfectly. Where a number of people lose credibility is when they do not make it clear that they take the miss seriously. Whenever you miss a target, make sure that you:

Insight

A large percentage of very capable leaders are reluctant to "toot their own horn," believing that "my work should speak for itself." Conversely, we are well aware of leaders who actively sell themselves, often when they have little of value to sell. Take a step back and empathize with the senior executives in the company. They have scores of leaders, most of whom are doing an above-average job. Excellent work that "should speak for itself" can be found everywhere. It is somewhat unreasonable to think that your work is so phenomenal that you will stand out to the entire executive team, isn't it? Help your leadership see what you and your team can do, know what you want, and understand what you are willing to do to get there.

- Accept that it is a miss, regardless of how small it is. If you minimize the miss, or describe it as "almost hitting my target," the executive you are speaking with may feel compelled to point out, "a miss is a miss." If you own the miss, there is little the executive can say, and they might be sympathetic: "Well it wasn't far off."

- Take 100% ownership for the miss, without explanations or justification. We have seen senior executives provide detailed analyses explaining why the miss occurred. Some leaders will experience this as a rationalization or justification, as though you were saying, "It's not really my fault." And all of them will be much more concerned with how you will change the situation.

- Explain clearly what you are going to do *differently* in the next month/ quarter that will change the situation going forward. This conveys the message that you have already understood the problem, and developed potential solutions. Executives almost always prefer to have you present one or more solutions to a problem than to drop the problem in their lap.

Find Ways to Innovate

While consistent delivery or over-delivering will be appreciated on its own, your managers and executives may not understand that you are ready to expand your responsibilities. Doing your work successfully without comment or fanfare is the safest approach. Organizations need people like you. Your boss and others will benefit from the work you do, supported by the work you did in Chapters 3–8 to focus your efforts on what they need. Organizations need people like you. This works if you're happy where you are, or with gradual expansion of your responsibilities, influence, and impact over time. If you want to take a more proactive approach, the following can be of help.

Most organizations in the current environment are focused on change, growth, and improvement. Business models, technology disruptions, COVID-19, and changing customer characteristics accelerate the pace of change. Helping your organization adapt and innovate can have a significantly positive impact for everyone. Put your hand up when opportunities come along to address a problem or streamline a process. Devote time to thinking about questions such as:

- Can we accelerate this process?

- Are there ways to simplify what we are doing so that progress and/or decisions can be made more efficiently?

- Why have we always done our work this way?
- What if we did not have the same constraints to our work—what could we accomplish?

Delivering Through Crises

Guest Contributor: Erica L. Spencer, Ph.D.

At the beginning of 2020, I set goals for the Learning and Development function that emphasized the continued digitization of our fundamental training content, as well as the implementation of our learning technology roadmap. We then cascaded these high-level goals to team members and defined specific initiatives and projects for each team. In March 2020, the coronavirus pandemic hit, causing an unprecedented impact on the hospitality industry. Given the impact, we were required to do more with less. We had to understand the constantly evolving recovery strategy and determine how learning and development could best support those efforts, while simultaneously supporting the digitization and technology efforts that were going to be critical moving forward.

As we dug into the details, we understood that COVID-19 had created a scenario in which we could accelerate and demonstrate the value of digital learning. We absolutely had to deliver training to associates on business-critical topics, such as the new cleanliness and safety protocols, as well as educate associates on how to work and manage teams in a virtual capacity. However, we no longer had the ability to deliver this training in-person. Through our focus on digitization of training, we created over 100 digital learning assets that supported our cleanliness efforts, which had been completed by over 430,000 associates within two months of launch. We also curated over 150 resources to support associates during their furlough, which were accessed by approximately 125,000 associates.

Our support also went beyond the typical learning and development initiatives. Our learning technology platform was used as the infrastructure to support work done by the broader HR organization, such as a Work Opportunities Site that showcased job opportunities for associates, as well as supported the data needed to support our reorganization efforts. Finally, the technology was leveraged to create an associate health screening program for associates who needed to return to the office.

As a result of the flexibility and commitment of our team, the learning and development organization was able to deliver what the organization needed during an extremely challenging time. This work was completely different than what we had planned, but we were still able to advance our overarching goals of digitization and learning technology. These efforts also served to stimulate change in the organization, getting our leaders and associates comfortable with and accepting of learning in a virtual environment.

Solve Problems for Your Manager (and Your Manager's Manager)

Your manager, and their managers, inevitably have problems that they have not been able to solve. These problems may interfere with achieving their objectives or may limit the amount of progress that has been made in their area of focus. Sometimes these problems are so deeply embedded in an organization that others do not see a way to change them. If you can solve these types of problems, your manager will know you are capable of taking on more responsibility.

> *Edwina was responsible for global customer support for the company's warranty services. The company had created their processes before many of the cloud resources were available and relied on spreadsheets and word documents to generate the necessary materials, including contract extensions, certified repair sources, and rebate checks. They had a large staff of people to provide these services, but they were still slow and error prone.*
>
> *She had joined the company from a fintech startup and was familiar with all of the cloud-based options available to solve these problems. Although she had been hired to run the customer support, she quickly developed a pilot program to use a cloud-based support system to meet some of these support needs. Within six months, she had reduced the turnaround time for contract extensions and rebate checks by 50%, and customer satisfaction ratings had increased significantly. In addition, she had retrained several people on both systems operation and analytics, so that she staff reductions were all voluntary retirements or transfers. Based on this, her manager got the company to commit resources to an enterprise-wide roll-out of the cloud-based system with significant efficiency gains and concomitant customer engagement.*

Start by anticipating their assumptions, objectives, and priorities. Integrate their preferences for how they receive information. Adjust, revise and practice as appropriate until you believe what you're saying and are confident in your analysis, recommendations, and messaging. Bosses care about both substance and style. Your confidence in yourself and what you're communicating will go a long way. Last, give your boss pre-reads that tell the whole story. They may or may not read your pre-reads but make the effort unless they tell you not to.

Address the Needs of Your Stakeholders

In Chapter 3, you identified who your key stakeholders are, and what their needs and objectives are. As you continue to deliver on your essential objectives, make sure your efforts include solutions that address the needs of your stakeholders. The Japanese term, *nemawashi*,* refers to the process of building the foundation for projects by talking to people, gathering input and support, and ensuring their concerns are integrated into your solution so that it is difficult for them to say, "no." Your job in this regard is twofold.

First, make sure you keep your understanding updated on a regular basis. We referred to this earlier as PQ. One client said, when discussing his stakeholders:

> *"Everyone has a certain agenda or objectives. Understanding their objectives is important to being successful. . . .Know who your stakeholders are, their concerns or what they hope to accomplish. I try to understand their concerns, so I can anticipate and address them. And you have to do it in a way that isn't dismissive, isn't confrontational."*

Second, make sure your stakeholders understand what you are trying to accomplish. The same client continued:

> *"When I first got here, people would propose a new product or idea by going into a meeting without any pre-meetings or discussions. They would encounter objections and issues, [and then] spend weeks or months reworking their proposal. I had them meet in advance with the key stakeholders to understand their primary concerns, so that we could anticipate and address these as part of our proposal."*

Adapt to the Context and Show Grit for the Mission

Building agility is a critical component of modern leadership, due to the VUCA nature of the current business environment.[ii] VUCA was coined by Warren Bennis and Burt Nanus in their classic text, *Leaders: The Strategies for Taking Charge*,[iii] referring to the Volatile, Uncertain, Complex, and Ambiguous environment of modern business.

---

*The term *nemawashi* refers to the method for transplanting trees, as a metaphor for taking the steps to create alignment and engagement with change while showing respect for the work that came before. According to Japanese gardening practices, successfully transplanting a tree involves cutting a large ball around the roots of the tree, and then introducing some of the soil from the new site so that the tree becomes accustomed to the new soil. After the tree has adapted, you can move the tree to the new location without causing unnecessary shock and trauma.

At the same time, it is essential that leaders and their teams maintain a relentless focus on their mission. Variations in the environment should not produce changes in the overall objectives of the organization. In fact, those variations can be seen as distractions that keep the team from achieving their objectives. Those variations can cause shifts in tactical methods of getting to the objective, but perseverance for the mission should remain steadfast.

Communicate Your Value

There are a variety of ways to communicate the value of your accomplishments and successes. How you choose to present your successes depends on the cultural context in which you work. For example, some companies encourage leaders to let their team members present their own work and demonstrate their knowledge and contribution. In others, you can only do this if they have sufficient presence, or practice enough to message what the executives want to hear. Other leadership teams do not want to hear from junior people at all. One company we consulted with insisted that the general manager of a business unit presents their quarterly review on their own, and expected those managers to know the answers to any questions the executive team raised.

Celebrating successes also varies from culture to culture. In some organizations, celebrations are actively encouraged. Anything from celebration dinners to pizza parties are supported and funded as a way of maintaining engagement and making team members feel valued. Other organizations discourage explicit celebrations, but may use financial rewards, performance awards, and other less overt ways to reward success. Regardless of the culture, there are a number of ways to demonstrate your value without being seen as boastful or self-aggrandizing.

Talk About The Work

There are a variety of ways to make your team known without it appearing to be self-serving. One way is to work with your manager and your team to find venues for talking about the work itself. Town halls are a common setting for talking about successful change initiatives or lean interventions. Joint team meetings can also be used to highlight cross-functional work performed by a workgroup drawn from several teams.

You can also send email blasts to senior leaders and other stakeholders to share the accomplishments of your team members. This works best when the work you are praising has direct implications for the person(s) you are sharing the information with. It is less effective when the accomplishments are more generic, or unrelated to particular strategic priorities. It is a good idea to thank your people for doing their work, but trumpeting their accomplishments are best when they are limited, targeted, and specific.

Bring Insights

One of the most common errors that junior people make when presenting to senior executives is forgetting to empathize with their audience. Instead, they think about themselves and what they think will put them in the best light. Unfortunately, that is usually what confuses others or puts them to sleep. Again and again, we see our clients present highly detailed decks that use multiple slides explaining how they gained the information, how hard they worked putting it all together, and only at the end telling what they have learned.

Empathy should tell you that executives have dozens of meetings a week, and are constantly bombarded with new information which they have to analyze. So, if you are one of the dozens of people who provide them with information, it will frustrate them no matter how valuable the information is. What executives really want is an insight: Why should all these data matter to me, and what can I, in my position, do with it?

If you point out something that has concrete implications for the executive, they are going to be very interested in how you got there. If your response to them is, "Let me tell you how I got there," of course you may fall back into the information dump. On the other hand, if you point out the key findings that led you to your insights, they are likely to ask, "OK, how do you know that?" Now, the executive has asked for the data rather than you forcing it on them. They are much less likely to flip through the deck, ask you to jump to a conclusion they themselves have drawn, or to check their phone for messages.

Synthesize Multiple Perspectives

In most organizational settings, differences of opinion are common, and in fact desirable. There is extensive research showing that openness to different points of view and different approaches are likely to produce better results than unilateral decisions. At some point, however, a decision has to be made. If you are the person who can synthesize multiple points of view, or seemingly mutually exclusive positions, you will be seen as someone with significant value.

One simple type of synthesis is "Both/And" thinking. Often, debates and discussions in business settings come down to whether you want goal X or goal

Y: strategic, or operational; collaboration or autonomy; continuity and change; agility or grit. The insightful executive finds a way to do both. When you start requiring yourself to find a solution that includes both sides of the coin, you are really showing your value.

Bring Your Team with You

Just as you have engaged your manager and your stakeholders, it is essential to bring your Main Team along with you. Your team, including indirect reports and business partners, is invaluable in helping to solve problems and demonstrate the capabilities of you and your team. Managers can describe the accomplishments of the people who work for them without fear of being seen to be egotistical or political.

> Deng was the business lead for a declining consumer product. A skilled strategist, he identified a new use case, updated branding, and modern channels for the product, and led his team to restart growth in a tough competitive market. An employee engagement survey showed that his team's scores were among the lowest in the firm, in large part because he was seen as self-aggrandizing and not standing up for his team. The coaching work immediately focused on what was missing for her team. Deng reframed his message from "I have solved the problem" to "My team has revamped the brand, and reignited energy for the product. I am only here because of the work they have done."
>
> In the first town hall Deng did after our work began, he spent ten minutes of a twenty-minute presentation describing the work of the individuals on his team without reference to his own insights, decisions, and clear focus. His manager almost immediately got feedback that Deng had made a sea-change that was welcomed.

It is generally acceptable to brag about others' work. Just don't brag about yourself. Talk about what others did, the impact of their work, and the learnings applicable to other areas.

Take Responsibility for Problems

Communicating your value should focus down as well as across and up. Your team, and other subordinates need to see your value as well. What they care about, however, is different than what your senior leaders care about. Fundamentally they want to know if they can trust you. Junior colleagues want to know that you value them, respect them, and think *they* have value. How do you do this?

One of the easiest ways is summed up by Harry S. Truman's belief that, "The buck stops here." A surprising number of managers will point out that a mistake was the fault of one of their team members, or (slightly more tactfully) that the team is still learning to use whatever tool they were using. Regardless of how you do it, if you blame your team for problems, they will describe you uncharitably as having "thrown them under the bus." You do not have to do this very many times for team members to stop trusting you. And that almost always gets around the organization. And more senior people will eventually see the problem as a management weakness rather than a skills deficit.

Back Up Your Team

Similar to taking responsibility for what your team produces, supporting decisions your team makes in public is an essential element of building trust and engagement. Whether you agree with the decision made is somewhat irrelevant. Defending your team on their choices tells them and others that you have their interests at heart.

What you do in private, when it is just you and your team, is another issue. Bad decisions due to sloppy thinking or shallow analyses should be addressed clearly and directly. Decision by indecision usually has to be addressed as well. But before you do that, make sure that you are open to hearing their views, and that you have created an environment where they can speak their minds and disagree with you with impunity.

Grow Your Value

Put Your Hand Up

You can certainly tell your manager that you are looking for additional challenges and want to take on expanded responsibilities. This makes it possible for them to look for cross-functional assignments, secondments, and committees where you can bring expertise to the table, or where you will learn new skills or competencies.

It is even more effective if you proactively look for ways to solve ongoing problems for the business, for your manager, or for stakeholders. Let your boss know that you want to help with a particular workstream. Ask them to assign this type of work to you. Consider volunteering for work that isn't immediately in your remit, but where you may be able to leverage generalizable skills like problem-solving or analytic skills.

Actively volunteering for new assignments can be somewhat riskier. The upside is that your boss will likely at least consider giving you more responsibilities. You're proving yourself more than capable of dealing with the responsibilities you've got and there's always more work that could be done.

The downside risk is that some may question your motives. If you're overdelivering and not talking about it, they assume you love the work itself. If you tell people you want more responsibilities, they may think you're overdelivering just to prove you deserve more responsibilities. Being explicit about wanting more responsibilities may prompt them to give you more. Just be careful. You may hate office politics, but you can be sure some people will play them with you.

Jump In and Fill the Gap

Sometimes it makes the most sense to jump in and solve a problem without waiting for permission or assignment. This runs some risk of annoying others or getting in the way of a colleague. If they are resentful or competitive, they can throw obstacles in your way. Nevertheless, this approach will probably be appreciated, and your message will be communicated, particularly if you are stepping into a crisis situation or if your manager is distracted by other crises.

One of the best ways to jump in and fill a gap is to work with your First Team (manager's direct reports) to create alignment, maintain priorities and focus, and inspire the team to persist when the manager is absent or unavailable. Think of this as being a leader among peers. This has to be done with a fair degree of political intelligence to be effective, of course. And when done over time, it has everything to do with leadership, and nothing to do with authority.

The classic example of how NOT to become a leader among peers was Alexander Haig's approach to being Secretary of State before and in the days immediately following the Ronald Reagan assassination attempt.[iv] Haig's infamous quote to the media was:

> *"Constitutionally, gentlemen, you have the president, the vice president and the secretary of state, in that order. . . .As of now, I am in control here, in the White House."*
>
> *Haig's problem was not just that he did not know the order of presidential succession. (He forgot about the Speaker of the House and the President Pro Tempore of the Senate, in that order). He apparently had been lobbying to take control of all aspects of foreign policy and asserting authority over other cabinet members. Instead of building relationships and aligning interests, Haig repeatedly forced others' hands, asserting without authority that he was responsible for various aspects of the executive branch.*

While the specific situation was quickly resolved, Haig continued to battle with other members of Reagan's cabinet, and ended up resigning after eighteen months, with a somewhat sullied reputation.

Leading a group of peers without line authority is perhaps the best example of having influence and impact. It requires several skills, including:

- Having a clear strategic understanding of the priorities of the First Team (your manager's direct reports).
- Having a history of listening to and sharing problem-solving with peers on the First Team.
- Having an authentic leadership style that clearly places the good of the organization at the top of your personal priorities (ego will definitely interfere with this).
- An ability to remain calm and resolute in the face of challenging situations (the opposite of Haig).

If you repeatedly take on particular additional responsibilities, eventually people will start assuming you're going to do them, and they will become part of your job.

Key Takeaways

You have to be responsible for your own growth. Sell your value to others without selling yourself by talking about the work, bringing insights instead of information, putting your hand up, and jumping in to fill gaps. These steps will help you take on more responsibility, expand your impact, and reap the benefits.

End Notes

[i] Ann Bengtsson, personal communication, Spring 2009.
[ii] Kaplan, B., & Kaiser, R. (2006). *The versatile leader: Make the most of your strengths without overdoing it* (J-B US non-franchise leadership) (1st ed.). Hoboken, NJ: Pfeiffer; Cleveland, S., & Cleveland, M. (2020). Toward leadership agility. In *Global issues and innovative solutions in healthcare, culture, and the environment* (pp. 1–13). Hershey, PA: IGI Global; Cleveland, M., & Cleveland, S. (2020). "Culturally agile

leadership: A relational leadership development approach." *International Journal of Public and Private Perspectives on Healthcare, Culture, and the Environment* (IJPP-PHCE), 4(1): 1–9; DeRue, D. S., Ashford, S. J., & Myers, C. G. (2012). "Learning agility: In search of conceptual clarity and theoretical grounding." *Industrial and Organizational Psychology,* 5(3): 258–279.

iii Bennis, W. & Nanus, B. (1985). *Leaders: The strategies for taking charge.* New York City: Harper & Row.

iv Allen, R. V. (2011, March 26). When Reagan Was Shot, Who Was "In Control" at the White House? Washington Post. Retrieved February 7, 2021 from https://www.washingtonpost.com/opinions/when-reagan-was-shot-who-was-in-control-at-the-white-house/2011/03/23/AFJlrfYB_story.html

PART IV

Plan B: If You Don't Want This Job, Find a Better Fit

CHAPTER 10

Getting Over the Job You Thought You Had

Managing Emotions and Moving Forward

"Life can only be understood backwards; but it must be lived forwards."

—Søren Kierkegaard

C oming to the realization that the job you have is not the job you thought it was can cause you enormous emotional turmoil. Hopefully, you realized this quickly and have not invested a lot of time and effort into the particular path you had been on. For many, however, this self-awareness may come after years of focused effort, and may disrupt plans and dreams you have had in place for a long time.

> *Frank had successfully moved from consulting to marketing to managing a small business unit within a global pharmaceutical firm.*
> *Quickly, however, Frank became mired in a range of difficulties in his new job. Two of his team members, including his operations head, were difficult to manage and resented his presence in "their" company.*

In addition, he identified a number of issues with logistics and supply chain that had not shown up under the previous general manager. Production slowed, and the FDA identified quality control issues at one of their facilities. The global head of operations demanded extensive detail on a weekly basis, and sent in a Six Sigma team from headquarters to evaluate their processes.

It became clear that Frank was unable to leverage his strengths as a strategic thinker and insightful analytic marketer in this job. Conversely, he disliked conflict management and over time grew tired with the endless focus on small details needed by both his manufacturing team and his senior management. Within a few months, he came to the realization that general management—certainly this general management job—was not all he thought it would be.

When a global marketing role with the new head of the International division became available, he raised his hand and moved over, where he returned to his high-performing status.

Frank's objective had been to become a CEO since he graduated college, and all of his moves had been taken with that in mind. He knew there was a problem, and knew it was his problem to solve, but he didn't know what he wanted to do about it.

Understanding Your Emotions

It is normal to experience emotional reactions when you are fired from a job.[i] But even if you decide yourself that your job is not for you, you are likely to go through a range of feelings that are common in situations of loss. Why? You have to let go of the job you thought you had, and the hopes, expectations, and dreams that came with it. The longer you held a role, and the more invested you are in the outcome, the more emotional work you may need to do.

In general, endings can be hard, even when you want them. At the simplest level, your habits and routines are upended. You no longer have a familiar set of actions and behaviors that shape your day-to-day life. Daniel Levinson[ii] described two broad phases in the course of adulthood. Most of our time is spent in structure-building periods, where you are consolidating your personal and social identity. Think of it as equivalent to painting, furnishing, and decorating your home.

Resilience

Guest Contributor: Leo F. Flanagan, Jr., Ph.D.

You're out. Whatever the exact case this chapter in your career is at an end. Your focus right now should be to learn and reassess.

The framework I use with people at this point is The Four Most Powerful Questions. A set of four questions that will motivate you to move forward and help you land well:

1. What do I want?
2. What am I doing?
3. How is that working?
4. What is my plan?

I ask my client to take the time, thought, and courageous honesty to address these four questions in relation to each of the following life arenas:

- Career
- Family
- Community
- Health
- Faith

Consider Jim a VP of Finance. Jim was focused on becoming a CFO, so he took a great CFO job, in a public company, headquartered in Chicago. The only hitch was that Jim's family lived in Scotch Plains, NJ. That family included his wife, a 17-year-old high school senior, and twin 15-year-old daughters.

No problem, Liberty International Airport was only 30 minutes from home with 90-minute flights to Chicago. Jim would rent a condo and fly home every Friday and back Sunday night. If one of the kids had an event, he would shoot home mid-week. He ran it by the CEO who famously said, "As long as the job gets done, I don't care where you lay your head down."

A month in, it was the opening game of son Doug's season as starting quarterback. Jim was on his way to catch a noon flight to get home in time for Doug's first game. As he was leaving, the CEO asked Jim "Hey, do you have a minute?" Jim barely made a 4 p.m. flight. He got to the game five minutes after it ended, so Jim was not there to see him throw two touchdown passes and rush for another touchdown.

Saturday morning, Susan had a 10 a.m. lacrosse game. At 9 a.m. the CEO's admin called. The CEO and three other executives were meeting in the office. Could Jim dial in? Of course, he could take the call at the field. What Susan saw during her game was her Dad pacing around the sidelines with his headphones on and gesticulating in the air. What the CEO heard was a lot of background noise and Jim not hearing people when they asked him questions.

Monday, the CHRO met with him and told him things just weren't a "good fit." Jim took a few days off to step back and answer The Four Most Powerful

Questions across all the life arenas. Here's how he answered them in regard to family.

Question: "What do I want with my family?"
Answer: "I want to be really connected to the kids before they are all off to college and out of the house."
Question: "What did I do to be really connected?"
Answer: "I took a super-demanding job half-way across the country and hoped I could still be connected to my kids."
Question: "How did that work out?"
Answer: "My kids and wife feel I let them down. It turned out that for the CEO 'getting the job done' meant being available and focused seven days a week. It didn't work at all—for anybody."
Question: "What's your plan?"
Answer: "Make location and manageable work demands a key criterion for my next role. Probably putting off being CFO for the next three or four years—at least with a major public company."

Jim took a job as controller of a pharmaceutical company 40 minutes from home. He invested in rebuilding his relationships with his wife and kids. He got to the office every morning by 7 a.m. to ensure he could leave in time for any of his kids' events, with the blessing of his CFO and the support of his admin.

There are also structure-changing periods, where your personal, professional, and social identities change dramatically—from student to worker, from spouse to spouse + parent, from employee to retiree. Think of this as equivalent to moving to a new home, in a new city, with a new job. Even if you want the change, it is a disruptive time, where your physical and emotional vulnerability increases.

There are lots of reasons why leaving a job may be difficult to deal with, even one of your own making. First, your self-esteem may be threatened. You may feel that the loss of their objective or a change in their professional trajectory is a failure. You can also react as though you have been treated unfairly, that your organization should have done more to help you succeed or help you remove institutional obstacles. It can also detract from a sense of agency, making you feel out of control in a major aspect of your life. And for many of us, work is a major source of social support. We build friends, relationships, and connection at work. When that is lost, it can result in feeling lonely or isolated.

Disbelief/denial   One of the most common reactions to discovering you are not in the job you want is disbelief. People spend time, from days to months, questioning their analysis of the current situation. The data can be quite clear, but some people go back and forth between acknowledging the reality of their situation and trying to revise the analysis. Others, of course, feel like their eyes have been opened, and never experience disbelief at all. Rather, they embrace the conclusion and immediately start moving forward. A sign that you are feeling disbelief is that you find yourself not taking the steps you need to take, or acting as though you do not need to make any changes.

Anger/disappointment Struggling with the need for a change can easily turn to disappointment or anger. "I've devoted years to this company (or manager), and when I hit some roadblocks, they throw me under the bus." And to some extent you are right. Your organization or your manager might be able to do more for you, but at the end of the day, that isn't their priority. Being successful as an organization is their priority. So, some degree of disappointment is justified. Signals that tell you anger may be getting in your way are when you find yourself thinking, "They should. . ." or "It's not fair. . . ."

Bargaining/yearning The experience of wishing things were different and trying to come up with a compromise solution is less common in job transitions than in other forms of loss. Thinking you can somehow trade your current situation for a prior environment may emerge if the job change disrupts your professional identity.[iii] For example, a lawyer coming to the realization that they do not want to be an attorney may trigger a yearning for "blissful ignorance."

Sadness/depression For many, simple sadness is unavoidable. Loss of a role, loss of a professional identity, feeling you have somehow failed are all triggers for sadness. It can last for a day, a week, or longer. Sadness shifts to depression, however, when your disappointment turns into feeling a lack of efficacy, power, or control over your life. It can also shift into depression if you begin to feel that you are not valued or cared for, or if you become disconnected from your main social network. People whose social connections and identity are primarily linked to work are more likely to feel depressed than those who have robust social networks outside of work.

To be sure, there is no right way to experience this type of loss. The notion that there are stages of grief has given way to a more flexible, adaptive framework for the emotions associated with loss and endings. You may experience one, several, or all of these emotions. For some, you may feel relief, leading you to open yourself to new possibilities. They may arise in a particular order, or you may shift back and forth among them on a daily or weekly cadence.

Guilt For others, however, realizing that you are in the wrong role, and possibly even the wrong profession, can lead to guilt that you are letting others down. Many people choose a career path because of personal or family expectations, or a responsibility to their community. When that commitment is not aligned with your values and ideals, however, success will be hard to find, and gratification will be even more remote. When you come to that realization, you may disappoint others; for some that can lead to guilt, which can then lead to depression.

Acceptance   For many people, accepting reality as it is and moving forward is one of the emotional states you may be able to adopt from the beginning. That is not how you will feel all the time, but most people feel more than one emotion at a time and certainly over periods of time. Acceptance means you are ready to take steps, or already have taken steps, to move on to the next chapter of your professional life. Over time, acceptance becomes the dominant emotional state, and the prior role becomes less and less salient as time passes.

Relief   Reaching the awareness that you are in the wrong job, and that you need to take steps to find something better lifts a conscious or unconscious burden. You may have been feeling the weight of being in the wrong job for a long time, which can be a source of stress and disquiet without you being able to pinpoint the source. Over time, many people feel enormous relief when they stop trying to fit in a job that is wrong for them.

Ambivalence   Technically, ambivalence is not a feeling—it is the manifestation of conflict—a combination of two opposing feelings, usually the desire to make a change and the desire to maintain the status quo. It is a normal life experience, and one we all experience. When the pros and cons of two options shift depending on how close you move to one choice or the other, ambivalence can become paralyzing.

Working Through, Around, and Over Emotions

Self-Understanding

The first way to manage the emotions around the decision to change roles, or change companies, is to accept that all of these feelings are normal. For most people, over a period of days and weeks, these feelings will resolve, and the motivation to move on will take over without you doing anything in particular. Feelings come and go, and you may feel guilt this morning, disappointment this evening, anger tonight, and acceptance tomorrow. Avoid making self-judgments and remind yourself that these feelings do not have to control how you act. You can feel guilty while exploring other opportunities and feel angry while talking to your manager about your options.

If you think that you are struggling with your feelings more than you would like, or that the feelings are interfering with your ability to make changes, there are a number of actions you can take to help bring them back under control. Many of these can be done on their own, or with the help of a coach, counselor, or therapist. You do not have to commit to a long relationship to work through these feelings. Sometimes as little as a session or two will help you to move forward.

Behavioral Methods

Building a pro/con list can be help to clarify why you have made this decision. In Chapters 2–4, we collected and analyzed an extensive amount of data. Having a simple summary of the reasons why you may stay in a job and why you might want to change can sometimes easily clarify your decision.

At the same time, you may want to move ahead regardless of your feelings. Treating your role change as a job in itself will help you move forward in spite of whatever feelings you have. Create a schedule for working on your options, and hold to it. If you are exploring opportunities while working, set a fixed amount of time each day you will devote to the effort. If you are in full-time search mode, get up at the same time every day, and create a daily routine. For example, one CEO who had left a role (not his choice) had a clear plan:

- 9:00–10:00 Review emails.
- 10:00–11:00 Read relevant news articles.
- 11:00–12:00 and 1:00–2:00 Identify people or events for networking.
- 2:00–5:00 Send emails and make phone calls.

Cognitive Methods

There are a wide range of cognitive coping techniques that help to manage emotions. First, pay attention to the internal dialogues that run through everyone's mind that relate to either who you are, how you act, or how you have been treated by others. Under normal circumstances, these internal dialogues are rational and not something you pay attention to. Under times of stress, however, this self-talk is both a reflection of and trigger for your emotional states. It can become overly black and white, or catastrophically exaggerated.

"I am really disappointed that this job is not what I expected," can become "I am such a disappointment; will I ever find a job I can be successful in?"

Sometimes just being aware of these thoughts can be enough to calm them down. When that brief thought says, "You are letting your family down," try saying it out loud. Bringing those thoughts into the light of day can help you realize that no one really feels that way. On the other hand, positive affirmations can be helpful in contradicting negative self-talk. Reminding yourself that, "I have been successful many times, and will be successful again," or "I deserve to have a job that I find fulfilling" can make all the difference.

Self-efficacy refers to the degree to which an individual feels they have agency or control in their lives.[iv] Building your sense of self-efficacy, through ongoing practice, stepwise accomplishments, or positive affirmations can increase your ability to succeed in finding a better role-fit. In simple terms, the higher your self-efficacy, the more likely you are to convert intentions into action.[v]

Interpersonal Methods

Using your social network of family, friends, colleagues, and mentors is one of the most effective methods of managing negative emotional states. In most cases, your family will be a great source of support and encouragement. Connecting with your social and professional networks is a close second. On LinkedIn, you will discover that almost everyone has changed jobs or left companies at some point in their lives. Seeking mentors or former managers who were supportive of you is a third source of guidance and encouragement.

Narrative Methods

Executive search professionals usually advise you to have a story to tell about why you are changing jobs. Having a coherent narrative that you can tell yourself and others as to how you got to your current situation is critical to finding a state of emotional equilibrium. Remember there is no single TRUTH as to how you got to where you are now. The story you use to explain your situation, however, can have a significant impact on your ability to accept and move forward.

Christopher sought out coaching because he found himself losing his temper with his colleagues in the refinery too often and too visibly. It was creating tension among his stakeholders and interfering with their work. He explained repeatedly how his co-workers disrespected him,

insulted him, or demeaned him, usually by turning in work product
that was below his standards.

Over a period of sessions, he began to understand that the quality
of work they produced had nothing to do with him. In reality, they
were not thinking about him at all, but rather focused on getting
through the overwhelming stack of materials on their desk. He did not
change his expectations for the quality of work, but he was able to stop
seeing it as a personal affront. This allowed him to find ways to man-
age their performance without getting quite so angry.

Take the time to craft several stories of your current situation. One story
may reflect your work's unfairness or the inherent difficulties your boss presented. Another story may show that the objectives of your manager are
different than your objectives; or that you discovered that your values are suf-
ficiently different that you have to make a different decision. Consider telling
your stories to a trusted friend and ask them what they think is most appropriate or most relevant to you.

Embrace a New Reality

The purpose of this chapter is to help you deal with the emotional reactions
you are likely to have if you have come to the realization that you are not in
the right job, or in the right company, given who you are and what matters to
you. There is a bright light at the end of the tunnel: A new role where your
strengths are valued and where you can use your influence to have a big impact
on the organization. Acceptance of the situation you are in, without undue
anger, resentment, or self-recrimination will help to get you to that place.

Key Takeaways

Get over the job you thought you had by understanding and accepting the
emotional side of your loss. Work through your own experience of the job
change, including disbelief/denial, anger/disappointment, bargaining/yearn-
ing, sadness/depression, and relief. This will help you accept and value who
you are and what you can do.

End Notes

[i] Gabriel, Y., Gray, D. E., & Goregaokar, H. (2013). "Job loss and its aftermath among managers and professionals: Wounded, fragmented and flexible." *Work, Employment and Society*, 27(1): 56–72; Papa, A., & Lancaster, N. (2016). "Identity continuity and loss after death, divorce, and job loss." *Self and Identity*, 15(1): 47–61.

[ii] Levinson, D. (1978). Seasons of a man's life. New York: Random House.; Sheehy, G. (1995). *New passages: Mapping your life across time.* New York: Random House.

[iii] Gabriel, Y., Gray, D. E., & Goregaokar, H. (2013). "Job loss and its aftermath among managers and professionals: Wounded, fragmented and flexible." *Work, Employment and Society* 27(1): 56–72.; Papa, A., & Lancaster, N. (2016). "Identity continuity and loss after death, divorce, and job loss." Self and Identity, 15(1): 47–61.

[iv] Bandura, A. (2001). "Social cognitive theory: An agentic perspective." *Annual Review of Psychology*, 52: 1–26.

[v] Maddux, J. E., & Gosselin, J. T. (2012). Self-efficacy. In Leary, M. R., & Tangney, J. P. (eds), *Handbook of self and identity* (pp. 198–224). New York: The Guilford Press.

CHAPTER 11

Negotiate for a Better Role Inside Your Organization
Find a Fit for Your Strengths and Influence

"You can't connect the dots looking forward; you can only connect them looking backwards. So, you have to trust that the dots will somehow connect in your future. You have to trust in something— your gut, destiny, life, karma, whatever."

—Steve Jobs

In Chapters 7 and 8, you created your Personal Strategic Plan to help you enhance your influence and impact in your current role. In this chapter, we help you create a Personal Strategic Plan designed to help you find a better fit for your strengths within your current organization. Your objective now is to discover a win-win by focusing on the intersection of the organization's needs and your strengths. A win for the organization means that your new role leverages your strengths in a way that better serves the organization. A win for you means that there is a better alignment between what they need you to do and what you want to do.

Your job is to identify the organizational priorities that you have the knowledge, skills, and interests to help solve. The approach we suggest here is to use the Personal Strategic Planning tool we described in Chapter 7, modified for changing roles to contribute to the organization going forward. We've included the tool at the end of this chapter.

Personal Strategic Plan for Role Change

In this version of the Personal Strategic Plan, you'll start with your personal mission, long-term objectives, and ideal job criteria, including values/guidelines/ways of working. Those three are your destination. Then you'll complete a personal situation analysis, including the organization's and your own personal current working mission and your strengths and growth opportunities. Finally, you'll lay out the strategies and then tactics to bridge the gap, improving the overlap between you and the organization.

Note that doing this on your own may present some challenges for you. Consider getting support and resources from others in your organization. You are likely to achieve much better results if you work with others, which can have the added effect of making your commitment to the organization clear. Your manager or your manager's manager is probably the first place to start. They have a broader view of the organization and may be able to help you identify where your strengths and preferences would fit best. In many cases, your manager wants you to succeed, even if that takes place outside their orbit.

A human resources business partner (HRBP) or human resources generalist (HRG) may also be a useful resource. In larger organizations, HRBPs may have access to career tools and learning systems that would facilitate your making a move to a more fitting team. In smaller organizations, they often have the ear of senior managers and can help pave the road to a better job for you.

If none of these options are available or feasible, consider getting a coach or consultant to help you with this.

Personal Mission and Long-Term Objectives

You defined your personal mission in Chapter 2. This will be particularly relevant to looking for a new role. Use your mission as a guidepost. Assuming you have decided to stay with the company, but you want a different job with a better fit, your mission will tell you what types of jobs you should consider. If your mission is to help people grow and develop, you may want to consider roles in human resources or communications. If you are more focused on solving interesting problems through technology, look for those types of opportunities. Be careful not to jump to a new role because someone else thinks it is a good fit for you. Your mission can help you think through your choices.

Your objectives should flow from your mission; they will help you refine your search. For some people, their long-term objectives are clear: "I want to be a CEO by the time I'm 40." Or, "I have no desire to manage people; I only want to be an expert in my field." For others, these are ill-defined or nonexistent. To the extent that you know your objectives, start with the furthest point ahead and work backwards. To the extent that you can, start laying out an entire career line. What do you want to achieve? Think about your professional life and about your personal life, and especially about the ways these are connected. If you don't have a career plan, start with what objectives you know of and work backwards to today.

Ideal Job Criteria

What is your ideal job experience? If you could wave a magic wand, what would that dream job look like? Explore what features are meaningful or important to you. Consider both the work itself, and the environment you work in. Make sure the job criteria you've come up with line up with your strengths and opportunities.

What are your technical or business interests? And what are your generalizable skills—strengths that are an important part of many jobs, such as quantitative analysis, problem-solving, managing people and relationships, or writing. What is the environment you like to work in? Would you prefer a fun-loving environment where colleagues are also friends? Or do you want to focus on work when at work, and keep your friends separate? Do you like to lead others, or be a member of a team? Do you like being responsible and accountable, or would you rather be in a supportive role? Consider all of these factors, as they are some of the most important elements of job satisfaction.

Your Personal Current Working Mission and Strengths and Growth Opportunities

You analyzed your current situation back in Chapter 2. That information is just as relevant at this point as it was when you first did it. Review these data, and see if you would make any changes now that you have decided you are not in the right job for you. Now that you are moving out of your former job, would you change any of your strengths or growth opportunities? Take the time to revise these self-assessments, so that you can think about your new opportunities with a clear, focused approach.[i]

Insight

When we are under stress, we tend to fall back on old habits and patterns. These may have worked for you in the past, but probably aren't appropriate for the current situation. Remember that people care mostly about what you can do for them. Lead with what you can contribute rather than with what they can do for you. Focus on—their needs, their objectives, their methods. Even though you are looking to help yourself, this is a great opportunity to practice being an other-focused leader. Think first about how to do good for others. Other-focused leaders instinctively do the one thing that can help everyone improve their ability to influence others—begin with empathy.

Take a Strategic Approach

The challenge is to either find or create opportunities where your skills and interests, and the needs of the organization, overlap. Citibank did a great job of this with Jane Fraser. Jane is the president of Citi and the chief executive officer of Global Consumer Banking. She is a member of Citi's Board of Directors, and she will succeed Mike Corbat as Citi's chief executive officer in February 2021. She will be the first female CEO in the firm's history.

> *Citi's Michael Klein spent several years trying to get Fraser to join Citibank, finally succeeding in 2004. He did this not because of her experience at Goldman Sachs, Assures Bursátiles, or McKinsey, not because of her Harvard MBA, but because of what she had learned researching and writing her book, "Race for the World: Strategies to Build a Great Global Firm."[ii]*
>
> *What she had learned was empathy.*
>
> *She researched this book by traveling around the world and interviewing McKinsey clients about their challenges. At the same time, she was working part time to spend time with her young children. The combination gave her a rare perspective range from global to as personal as it gets.*
>
> *Then Citi moved her through a series of positions that allowed her to build knowledge and skills, heading up client strategy, mergers and acquisitions, the Private Bank, CitiMortgage, US Consumer and Commercial Banking, Citigroup Latin America, Global Consumer Banking.*

She will take over as CEO with the ability, knowledge, and skills required to steer the bank out of the pandemic and through the uncertain future we all have to deal with.

You may not be on target to be the next CEO of a global organization, but the point is still the same: You need to take the initiative to acquire new skills and experiences. The majority of growth opportunities come from on-the-job experiences. Not just new jobs, but project-based assignments, committees, or networking opportunities can all help you develop. You can also read, take a course, or find a mentor. Take charge of your own career, and do not wait for your company to provide the opportunity. If you need to learn a new skill, enroll in the appropriate online courses or programs, read the literature, or find another way to learn it.

Look for Tactical Opportunities

Creating and finding opportunities is easier if you and your boss have agreed on a longer-term strategic plan for you. If they agree that you should acquire knowledge and skills in certain areas over time and one of those opportunities comes up, it's easier for them see the long-term versus short-term trade-off.

Taking advantage of tactical opportunities is trickier, especially if it means your boss loses some or all of your immediate contributions. And even trickier if your main driver is getting away from your boss.

Keep your eyes open for appropriate project work, training programs, and assignments. These are the same components you thought about in your long-term career discussion. The difference is that those were all about building your capabilities. When you're talking about immediate opportunities you need to be able to add value while you are building capabilities.

Projects are the easiest. Many of them will fit within your current remit. That means that putting you on these doesn't cost your boss anything. Even if they don't fit exactly, they may not require all of your time. You can keep doing the job your boss needs you to do now while building capabilities. (And keep working for your current boss, assuming that's a good thing.)

Training programs are a little trickier as they force a long-term strength-building versus short-term contribution trade-off. The good news is that they are time-bound. Look for programs that take the least amount of your work time, or get the buy-in of your organization. For example, it's going to be far easier to get your boss to support a training program you do five Saturdays in a row than five workdays in a row.

New Role, New Manager

New assignments reporting to a different boss pose the biggest trade-off. Your manager has to value the long-term benefit to the organization more than losing you as an employee. Over time, those are the people that fuel the best organizations, but they tend to be in the minority unless the company you work for explicitly incorporates role changes as a part of their organizational talent planning.

These types of jobs might include other jobs in the same function. Or, they might include a new experience altogether.

If you trust your manager, broach it gently with them. Let them know that you have the sense that you could be doing much better if you were doing what they really need (job X.) However, you think you could bring even more to a role like role Y. Ask where they think you can make the greatest contributions. Raise this as questions, rather than statements. Be clear that you want to do as much as possible for them, for the firm, for customers and others. If they agree, ask about next steps.

If they disagree, consider revising your analysis or talking to your skip-level manager or someone else you trust.

In any case, keep doing your job well until you move to another job. Maintaining good relationships with your bosses can benefit you in the future. It's a small world.

Talent Scouting

Guest Contributor: Kerry Bessey

Before joining Memorial Sloan Kettering, I worked for a global telecommunications company with over 90,000 employees. That taught me that part of a leader's role is to be both a talent scout and developer for the entire organization, not just one's own group. We regularly discussed people's transferable skills. We wanted to ensure that those skills enabled them to be put in key stretch assignments, rounding out their "portfolio" and applying them in different size businesses, as well as businesses in different stages of their lifecycle (start-ups, turn-arounds, mature).

This principle can be applied in smaller environments as well. In enterprises that don't have the scale to do planned moves between businesses or divisions, it requires focusing on the skills components of various roles rather than the experience component. Shortly after my arrival at Memorial Sloane Kettering, I needed to replace my head of compensation and benefits. The position description called for deep compensation knowledge, knowledge of physician compensation practices, benefits, and was a key interface with the Board of Directors. Knowledge of our complex organization would clearly be a plus as well.

With no internal candidates within the HR organization, I started thinking about senior leaders internally. Who had analytical and quantitative skills and board experience? Were any of them ready for a move? Who might be willing to take on a new role with a steep learning curve?

I conducted a number of "get to know you" conversations with other senior leaders, and kept those criteria in mind. I identified a terrific candidate who was our compliance and audit leader. In a somewhat unusual move for our culture, she agreed to take the leap and come work for me. This was courageous on her part on several levels. She took a risk that could, of course, have failed (spoiler alert: it didn't!) and she stepped back from being the head of her own division to come work in a larger division where she was no longer the division head. In the end, it was a win for her by reenergizing her and helping her gain transferrable new skills. It was also a win, for the organization, who benefited from her deep knowledge and relationships. After a few years she again moved, this time for promotion in hospital administration.

Building a Network Beyond Your Direct Line

Part of managing your own career is doing your own marketing—especially if part of what you're trying to do is to get away from your boss. In any case, think AIDA—Awareness, Interest, Desire, Action.

Awareness

Your target audience is everyone who can make or influence decisions about your next role—including your HR business partner and other neutral third parties.

Your first job is to do your current job well. Remember the insight that a lot of leaders say, "My work should speak for itself." They're not entirely wrong. Your work has to speak for itself. You're just going to give it some other channels in which to speak.

Tip for Leaders

Bosses who are unwilling to support you for advancement put you in a Catch-22 situation. You need their support to get out. And you need to get out because they won't support your getting out. This is why it's always important to build a network that extends beyond just your boss.

It starts with building awareness of the work. Note we didn't say "building awareness of you." It's not about you at this point. It's about the work. Build awareness by telling others in the organization about the good work done by your teammates so they can learn from it, duplicate it, and praise the people you're working with. It's not a quid pro quo. Just doing that builds awareness in what you're getting done.

Interest

Interest is shared. If you show interest in what others are doing, they are far more likely to show interest in what you're doing.

Make it a point to learn about what's going on in areas adjacent to yours—particularly areas in which you might want to work on projects or do future assignments.

Call people up and ask them to tell you what they are doing. So many people have so many pressure-filled meetings in which others are judging them that someone just asking to learn can be a breath of fresh air. Don't judge. Don't offer advice. Just show your interest. Just learn. Be that breath of fresh air. Some, but not all, will ask about what you're doing. When they do, tell them. But focus on the work and others' accomplishments. It is not about you. It's about the work.

Desire

Desire is triggered by an unmet need. No one's going to ask you to join a project or take an assignment if they're not aware of you. And they are more likely to ask if they have gotten to know you a little.

Your organization is going to evolve on a continuous basis. Needs will pop up. You will be the wrong resource for most of them. But you will be right for some of them. And it's going to be that much harder for your boss to block you making a move if someone else is asking for you specifically. And it's much easier for you to go to your boss with another opportunity that you think you should take, no matter how much you'll miss working for them (whether or not that's actually the case).

Action

Of course, the bottom line is getting someone—you or someone in your company—to take action. The case below shows how George ended up in Coke-Japan.

Coca-Cola's Japanese bottlers came to the UK to learn about private labels. My boss was supposed to present to them, but got called away at the last minute. Instead, I was asked to fill in. Luckily, one of the Coca-Cola Japan executives stopped by my office the day before to warn me about what to expect.

"They are going to be early. And half of them will look like they're asleep five minutes into your presentation. They are not. The most senior people close their eyes to take in the gestalt of the meeting while their junior people take notes."

Sure enough, someone walked into my office at 9:45 the next morning to tell me that all the bottlers were assembled and ready for their 10:30 meeting. The executive had prepared me well. The meeting went well. The bottlers were interested in what I had to tell them.

A couple of months later, the Japanese leadership team told the company's senior leadership that it needed ten executives to move to Japan to help them accelerate progress. Company leadership told them to pick any ten anywhere in the world and they would be transferred.

I was one of the ten they identified. My boss had to let me go (to Japan).

Key Takeaways

If you like the organization you are in, negotiate for a better role. Find a fit for your strengths and influence by reconfirming your own personal mission and long-term objectives, your ideal job criteria, your values and ways of working. Then re-examine your situational analysis to develop strategies to identify and improve the overlap between your own and the organization's missions.

Download an editable worksheet at **www.BermanLeadership.com/ InfluenceandImpact**

Worksheet 11.1   Personal Strategic Plan™—For Role Change

Personal Mission/ Long-Term Objectives:	
Ideal Job Criteria and Values/Ways of Working:	
Situation Analysis:	
Organizational Mission:	
Personal Working Mission:	

	Strategies to Identify and Improve Person/Organization Overlap:		
Role Change Strategy	Tactics/Actions	Success	Date
Focus Area 1			
Focus Area 2			
Focus Area 3			

End Notes

[i] Miller, L. E., & Jackson, B. (2007). *UP influence, power and the U perspective: The art of getting what you want* (1st ed.). New York: Your Career Doctors Press.

[ii] Bradt, G. (2020, October). How Naming Jane Fraser CEO Advances Citibank's Client Focus. Forbes. Retrieved February 7, 2021 from https://www.forbes.com/sites/georgebradt/2020/09/10/how-naming-jane-fraser-ceo-advances-citibanks-client-focus/?sh=2282e4f21e97.

CHAPTER 12

Make a Plan to Move On

Sometimes You Need a Fresh Start

"Life is a series of natural and spontaneous changes. Don't resist them—that only creates sorrow. Let reality be reality. Let things flow naturally forward in whatever way they like."

—Lao Tzu

This chapter is for those who have decided they need a fresh start in a new job with a new manager in a new company. The question is how to get from where you are to where you want to be. Do you look for a job while still employed? Do you take "a package" or quit outright to devote 100% of your time to looking for a job? What do you do first, next, after that?

Looking for a job is stressful. It takes time, effort, and an ability to tolerate failure multiple times. After all, every time you apply for a job, at each step in the process, you feel like you have failed until you take a job. You feel like you have no control over your career. It's stressful whether you look for a job while still employed or not.

If you are still employed, you have the additional stress of leading a double life. You still should be giving 100% of your best effort to your job, teammates, and employer (so they do not think you are looking for a job). At the same time, you are planning to deprive them of their best asset—you. You're going to go to work on looking for a job after you've completed the work of doing your job.

Insight

Because the risk of feeling like a failure is so great, and so natural, it is important to find as many ways as possible to establish control over your situation as you look for a job. Remember (or look at) the cognitive methods we described in Chapter 10. Remind yourself that you deserve to have a good job that reflects your skills and experiences. Reward yourself for taking the right steps, rather than just for getting the job. Remember, you will submit 100 résumés, in order to get 20 calls, in order to get five interviews, in order to get one job offer. Each of those is a success, because it took you toward your objective.

If you are unemployed, you have the stress of not having a paycheck. You have the stress of not being able to answer the question, "What do you do?" You have the stress in job interviews of explaining why you lost your last job. You have the stress of not being able to leave your house and go to work. (Although, at the time of writing, this is the midst of the COVID-19 pandemic in the US, and most people are not able to leave their homes and go to work.)

Treat looking for a job as a job. If you are unemployed, approach it as a full-time job. If you are employed, think of it as your second job. The more time and effort you put into the work, the more likely you are to find a better job faster. There are several parts of the job search that make it easier or more effective:

- Create a routine. Start at the same time every day. Work until the same time every day. Get dressed for work—you will feel better about yourself and you will be prepared if a call or interview happens unexpectedly.

- Leverage your network. You are much more likely to get a call-back or an interview if you are making a warm call—someone referred you to the hiring manager or HR.

- Set reasonable expectations. Depending on your level in an organization, it can take a long time to get a job. Most senior executives we have worked with have spent a year or more looking for a job before finding one that fits them and is interested in them.

- Remember job-hunting is a statistical matter. Just like baseball players are doing well if they get on base only 25% of the time, you are doing well if you get a few phone calls in response to dozens of submissions. According to anecdotal reports, the likelihood of getting a call-back on a résumé submission to an online site is below 2%. There are techniques for better performance, but the result is that you have to submit a lot of résumés online to get a job.

- Unless you desperately need a job—to pay your mortgage, rent, or food bills—try not to take a job simply because it was offered. Make sure it meets your professional and personal needs as well as your financial needs.

Position Yourself to Create Value for Others

Know yourself. We reviewed this in Chapter 2. Knowing who you are includes knowing your strengths, development areas, values, challenges, and long-term objectives. These are essential to finding a new job that fits with who you are. If you do not recall what you did, go back to the worksheets from Chapter 2 and review them.

When you are looking for another job, you are a sales representative. You are representing yourself. Good salespeople know that it's not about you. You sell based on the benefits to the purchaser. Potential employers want to know how you can help them create value, and why they should believe you. This is the core of your elevator pitch and résumé.

Think through your own positioning. Be clear about who your target audience is: What types of organizations and people might need you? Be clear about your value: What type of job might you do for them? Consider the benefits you offer: What can you provide for them? Think about your method of persuasion: What are the evidence-based reasons they should believe you? Make that positioning, especially the benefits, explicit in your cover letter, your résumé, and your elevator pitch.

One of the most common mistakes people make when they are looking for a job—particularly when they are not currently working—is they present themselves as broadly as possible. The objective is to cast the widest net possible in the hopes that one will be a success. People do this because of anxiety: They are afraid of missing a job they might have been hired for. Despite its obvious appeal, this is rarely the best approach. Professional athletes know that the recipe for success is to play where they have a strategic advantage, and consistently do what they do best rather than trying to be equally good at everything.

Our advice is to only apply for the jobs that fit your strengths and talents, and nail that job interview. Applying for jobs that are not in your sweet spot can add to your demoralization and may even annoy people who are helping you find a job. Just as organizations perform best when they make the strategic decisions of "Where play, how win," you will do best by being focused and clear on your unique selling points. Invest heavily in opportunities that are most right. Walk away from the rest.

We call the former the 90/10 candidate, because they miss on 90% of the jobs, but nail 10%. We call the latter the 60/40 candidate, because they only miss on 40% but they usually come in 2nd on 60%. When you are a 60/40 candidate, you have to position yourself toward the mean, so you appeal widely. When you tend toward the mean, you round your edges, so you offend fewer people. You are more acceptable, but feel less passion so inspire less passion about yourself. As a result, you make the cut to be a final candidate for jobs more frequently than others, but often come in second place.

Sometimes we fall into this slowly, telling ourselves, "Well, that isn't ideal, but more job offers give me more options" or "I'm sure once I get there, they will be more flexible about the role." This tendency comes from anxiety. Fight it. You are already leaving a job that is not a good fit for your strengths and preferences. In addition, it is rare for people to get more than one job offer at a time, unless you have really special skills and experiences. Every job offer should be a yes/no decision that stands on its own. Last, as we've pointed out repeatedly in this book, organizations are not predisposed to flexing to meet your needs.

The difference is focus and the courage to talk about what's most important and walk away from opportunities where the fit is less clear.

> *During a team coaching engagement, Erica identified a member of the team, Sami, who was a source of frustration to several team members. Sami rarely did paperwork, he overreached on issues that did not concern him, and was often unresponsive to others on the team. When I raised this to Erica, she explained, "Sami is not very good at several of the things his peers want from him. I knew that would be an issue when I hired him. But I brought him in because he has one of the best legal minds I have ever worked with. When I need someone to get me through a complex deal, he always finds a solution that is to my advantage. I can find people who can do paperwork for him and pull him away from non-legal projects. But his strengths are extremely hard to replace."*

Sometimes you do want to move toward the mean, but not when it comes to positioning yourself and your career. Be known for something. Invest in it, get better at it, and claim your expertise. Talk about it and use it as much as possible. And look for ways to manage the rest.

Uncover and Create Options

Uncover Options That Already Exist

The key to creating options is to leverage your network of relationships. Create a networking plan with different amounts of time and effort for each of three tiers. Implement your plan with discipline, rigor, and follow-through.

The first tier is the people who know people who need you. The majority of jobs are found through these connections. This includes all of your former managers, subordinates, peers, customers, vendors, and teachers. It can also include people from volunteer activities, boards, or committees. When you speak with these people, make sure the last question you ask them is, "Is there anyone you know that you think might be good for me to speak with?" Much of this can be done through technology like LinkedIn and Facebook, but we recommend you pick up the phone or have meetings whenever possible.

The second tier is personal connections, although fewer roles are found through non-work contacts. Still, these relationships can often yield surprising results. Connect or reconnect with classmates, fraternity/sorority connections, religious affiliations, professional contacts such as lawyers and brokers, and even your children's school and sports connections.

> A colleague of ours was looking for a job. One Saturday morning, while attending his daughter's soccer game, he started talking with the father of another girl on the team. After a few pleasantries, the other man asked him about his work. Our colleague explained he was let go after a merger. That other father turned out to be the head of HR for a company and invited him in for exploratory interviews the following Thursday.
>
> Unbeknownst to our colleague, that Monday that company had a melt-down with its largest customer. On Tuesday, senior leadership met and decided they need to find some people with better solution-focused client management experience. When our colleague showed up for his exploratory interview on Thursday, he told them he's been finding custom solutions for large, complex clients for the past decade. They hired him to manage the team responsible for their $3B in annual business with Walmart.

Recruiters, job sites, and advertisements are a third tier of job search. These are far less likely to yield results, unless you have a specific skill or experience that stands out in the job description. Do not close this door, but, do not confuse it with the other tiers.

Create Options That Should Exist

There are a few ways to create new options. Richard Nelson Bolles wrote *What Color Is Your Parachute?* 50 years ago, and it is still considered the best job search book on the market.[i] He recommends conducting "informational interviews" with a wide range of people, including businessmen who are written up in the local paper, or small businesses that do work in your field. Note these are not job interviews, or even job explorations. They should be completely focused on the person you are interviewing: What they do, what problems they have, and how they have succeeded in their business.

Prepare for and Handle Interviews Better than Anyone Else

The purpose of a job interview is to convince the hiring manager that you are the best candidate for the job. Period. Candidates for jobs need to convince hiring managers that they can do the job (strengths), will love the job (motivation), and will be a good colleague (fit), better and more than any other candidate.

Now is not the time to figure out if you really like the company. That comes later. It is your responsibility to convince the people interviewing you that:

1. Your strengths are what they need to solve their problems as evidenced by the examples you cited. You can do this job.

2. You are motivated by things you will do in this job, the impact you will make on others, and the effect that will have. You're going to love this job.

3. You are value-additive to the culture. You do not need to be the same as the organization you work in, but you have to be able to work with the people in the organization. You want them to be inclusive of your style, but you also have to be able to adapt to theirs.

Start by researching the company and conduct as much of a 5Cs analysis as you can: Capabilities, Customers, Collaborators, Competitors, and Conditions. In the internet era, you can learn a great deal about a company before you get there. And do not be afraid to look up your interviewer on social media, if you know who they are. They will likely have checked you out.

Just because you are being interviewed does not mean you have to do all the talking. Make sure you convey to the interviewer that you listened to them, and that you understand them. Ask them questions about their work, the job, and themselves, particularly if they are the hiring manager. Some of the best interviews are ones where the interviewer does as much talking as you do. Important things to ask about, to understand the job opportunity, include: The mission, or what the opportunity to create value is; what success looks like; and what skills, knowledge, and experiences are most important for the job.

Behavioral interviews are becoming more and more common. In these types of interviews, you are asked to describe a specific situation in which you did something—solved a knotty problem, broke through resistance, collaborated, drove results, and the like. Think through stories that reflect your strengths and capabilities and be prepared to describe these situations. The more specific and detailed your story, the better. Be sure to describe what *you* did as well as what the team as a whole did. And the more these stories fit with your 5C's analysis, the better.

What happens when you are responding to questions from someone who hasn't been trained in behavioral interviewing? Manage the questions in a way that makes the interviewer feel good about themselves and what they uncover about you. To do this successfully, follow three simple steps: Think—Answer—Bridge:

- It is fine to take time to think about your answer. Do not take minutes, but a few seconds are fine. If you do, you are likely to answer more than what was asked; you will answer the true underlying question (strengths, motivation, or fit).

- Answer the question asked. You want to answer their questions, as long as they are legal and appropriate. This tells them that you heard and cared about their question. Not answering their question says either you are not prepared or do not care about them.*

- Bridge from your basic answer to something valuable about you—either strengths, motivation, or fit—depending upon the true underlying question. Bridging is an art. You must connect the dots between your response to the question asked and the answer to the underlying true question. Bridge too far and your interviewer can't make the leap. Find a link—a connection—and use it to get from where you are to where you need to be.

If, for example, you're asked about your volunteer work with underprivileged children and you want to talk about your communication strengths, you might say something like:

*There are definitely some questions that you should not answer. Every state, and the Equal Employment Opportunity Commission, and the federal government have identified questions that they consider to be discriminatory. For example, in New York State you are not allowed to ask someone's current or prior salary, as it promotes pay disparities. And some interviewers ask odd or bizarre questions. We still recommend you use the Think—Answer—Bridge approach.

What I most enjoy about working with children is being able to make a contribution to people with a very different background than mine. Connecting with people with different backgrounds and communicating with them is one of my strengths. For example, in my last corporate job I once. . .

See the bridge? Working with children to connecting with people to communication.

The closer you get to the final interview, the more you need to convey your motivation for this job in particular, rather than your skills for the job. Skills are typically what are covered in the initial interviews. And you may not know enough about the culture to be able to influence that decision. Being clear and specific about why you want this job tells the interviewer two things: what matters to you, and that you have been listening to what the job really is.

The most important thing to convey from a cultural perspective is agility. Learning agility or cultural agility are important, generalizable skills that allow you to interact with a variety of people in a variety of ways. It is not about being a chameleon, but rather about learning not only how people communicate verbally, but how they communicate nonverbally. Be clear about who you are, of course, but show a willingness to be able to work within the organization as it is.

Since there are only three interview questions,[ii] prepare answers in advance and bridge to them:

- Will you love the job? What you value and enjoy.
- Can you do the job? Your technical, management, and leadership skills.
- Will we be able to tolerate you? Your social skills, emotional intelligence, and cultural agility.

Time to Move On

Guest Contributor: Barry A. Schub

Several years ago, I decided to retire from a senior job that was extremely challenging and satisfying. I knew that I wanted more free time but beyond that I had little in the way of concrete plans on how I would actually spend my time.

After a tough initial period of adjustment, I have found a good balance of family, consulting, coaching, charitable, and personal interest activities to keep me stimulated and engaged while also having the free time I had sought. Some observations:

Adjusting can be tough. The biggest initial change was not having a built-in network of bright people around for daily interactions. Re-creating a similar level of interaction outside an office is challenging and time-consuming.

Opportunities await. Don't try to make detailed plans on how you will find specific opportunities to stay engaged. Your network is invariably larger, deeper, and more varied than you realize. Reaching out to stay in touch will invariably lead to conversations about ways in which you can help. All of my current engagements emerged this way. One key activity even arose with a colleague's husband who I had never met. Your biggest risk might be finding too many engagements and not having enough free time.

Leadership will take new forms. After many years in senior positions, it is easy to forget that many people look to you for decisions and direction. I now have a series of roles that allow me to fulfill several aspects of my former leadership roles:

- Problem-Solving—several consulting assignments allow me to perform the "figure it out" part of leadership.
- Development—my mentoring and coaching allows me to continue the aspect of leadership that I probably enjoyed most—helping talented people improve and thrive.
- Decision-Making—this is by far the hardest part of the transition. The habit and inclination to be directive needs to evolve to a form of influence management. This has been a challenging and sometimes frustrating change.

Most important, follow your passions. I am on an investment committee overseeing the endowment of a charity I care about. We have always supported the arts, and I am now able to attend lectures on my areas of deepest personal interest and passion.

I have the opportunity to help friends and colleagues with current or new job challenges and opportunities. These conversations are stimulating, satisfying, and can also lead to new contacts.

And best of all, I have much more time for our growing family, travel, and taking care of myself.

Net—RELAX. You will find plenty of ways to stay engaged and enjoy your new and very different life. Don't try to plan everything, and keep your mind open for new ways to apply your skills and experience.

Sell First, Then Buy

You can't turn down a job you haven't been offered. So, maintain a single-minded focus on selling until you are offered the job. Do the real due diligence after the offer, especially around organization, role, and personal risks.

For Zappos' CEO Tony Hsieh (who sadly died as we were writing this book), the most important decision was where to play. He learned that playing poker. He applied it at Zappos. It's critical for onboarding. In Hsieh's own words:[iii]

Through reading poker books and practicing by playing, I spent a lot of time learning about the best strategy to play once I was actually sitting down at a table. My big "ah-ha!" moment came when I finally learned that the game started even before I sat down in a seat.

In a poker room at a casino, there are usually many different choices of tables. Each table has different stakes, different players, and different dynamics that change as the players come and go, and as players get excited, upset, or tired.

I learned that the most important decision I could make was which table to sit at.

Take Charge of Your Own Onboarding

We know that at least 40% of new senior leaders fail in their first 18 months.[iv] Many of these failures are the result of choosing the wrong table and stepping on an organizational, role, or personal land mine that should have been seen before accepting the job.

Once you've been offered the job, do your due diligence to make sure it is right for you.[v] This involves mitigating organizational, role, and personal risks by answering three questions:

- What is the organization's sustainable competitive advantage? (To get at organizational risk.)
- Did anyone have concerns about this role; and, if so, what was done to mitigate them? (To get at role risk.)
- What, specifically, about me, led the organization to offer me the job? (To get at personal risk.)

Organizational Risk

Mitigating organizational risk elements involves making sure the organization has a clear strategy, the resources to fund it, and the people to carry it out. You know some of this from your 5Cs analysis we discussed earlier. Now that you have been offered the job, invest the effort to see what new things you can learn. As Christopher Frank and Paul Magnone describe in their book, *Drinking from the Fire Hose*, pay special attention to what surprised you.[vi] In particular, you need to understand all these in the light of the specific job you've been offered.

Role Risk

To mitigate role risk, make sure that the job is well defined, has clear deliverables, and has the necessary tools, systems, and budget to do it well. In particular, look hard at peers. The most likely place for there to be issues are peers who think your new job overlaps with parts of theirs. Other places to look are in the specifics of the job:

> Nadine was offered the role of chief diversity officer. It was a stretch assignment for her, and she was flattered that she got the offer. It also accelerated her career plans by several years. On the advice of a colleague, she asked two questions: Who will I report to?; and, What is the budget for the role? She discovered that she would be reporting to the head of Human Resources, who reported to the chief administrative officer, who reported to the US CEO. Her budget, it turned out, was not determined. Her first job would be to create a budget and submit it for the next budget cycle. She correctly saw the combination of these data as major warning signs, and declined the job.

Personal Risk

The objective in mitigating personal risk is to determine for yourself if your strengths, motivation, and style are a match for what is required to deliver the expected results. Knowing what you know, would you hire yourself for the job? If there are significant differences, probe and explore, and keep the option of walking away open in your mind. If you feel like it is a stretch, or will challenge you, don't get scared. But there is a difference between challenging yourself and trying to do a job you aren't really qualified for. Saying "No" to a job because you do not think you are right for it is one of the best career moves you can make.

Now What?

With those answers in hand, you can then decide if you have a low level of risk that requires no extraordinary actions, manageable risk that you'll manage as you go, mission-crippling risk that you must resolve before going forward, or insurmountable barriers requiring you to walk away.

Key Takeaways

Sometimes you need a fresh start. When you do, leave strong, minimize the damage, leverage your networks. Know yourself. Then position yourself to create value for others. Uncover and create options, manage interviews and your own onboarding.

End Notes

[i] Bolles, R. N. (2019). *What Color is Your Parachute? 2020: A practical manual for job-hunters and career-changers* (Reprint ed.). Berkeley, CA: Ten Speed Press.

[ii] Bradt, G. (2011, April 27). Top Executive Recruiters Agree There Are Only Three True Job Interview Questions. Forbes.com. Retrieved February 7, 2021 from https://www.forbes.com/sites/georgebradt/2011/04/27/top-executive-recruiters-agree-there-are-only-three-key-job-interview-questions/?sh=4b632096f35c

[iii] Bradt, G. (2011, April 10). Be like Zappos' Tony Hsieh—Answer Three Key Onboarding Due Diligence Questions. Retrieved February 7, 2021 from https://www.forbes.com/sites/georgebradt/2011/08/10/be-like-zappos-tony-hsieh-answer-three-key-onboarding-due-diligence-questions/?sh=7360f270b5bb

[iv] Masters, B. (2009, March 30). Rise of a Headhunter. Financial Times. Retrieved February 7, 2021 from https://www.ft.com/content/19975256-1af2-11de-8aa3-0000779fd2ac

[v] Bradt, G. (2011, April 27). The Importance of Due Diligence Before Accepting a Job. PrimeGenesis. Retrieved February 7, 2021 from https://www.primegenesis.com/our-blog/2011/04/the-importance-of-due-diligence-before-accepting-a-job/

[vi] Frank, C. J., & Magnone, P. F. (2011). *Drinking from a fire hose: Making smarter decisions without drowning in information.* NY: Portfolio.

PART V

Helping Others Build Their Influence and Impact

CHAPTER 13

A Primer
for Managers

How to Coach Your Employees to Increase Their Influence and Impact

"After 23 years of work. . .when I look back. . .what I remember and get the most joy from [is] the team members I have helped finding the right career track, or helped to get more pay for their great work, or conversely, those fewer I have pushed gently to find a more suitable career. Each time, it was a lot of time and intense discussions, but it was always worth it."

—Elizabeth Ling Decitre

Whether you are a manager of a small team, or the leader of a whole business, the objective of this chapter is the same. For you to be successful, your people—one, ten, or ten thousand—need to be successful. Our guidance here is intended for you in relation to your direct reports or your skip-level report (one layer down). But the same guidance applies even if you are focused on someone deep in your organization. Help them to understand what the job entails, and what the culture expects, so that they can do the work you need from them *the most*.

Recall our fundamental premise from the first chapter: Many people who are struggling in their job are not focused on the most essential, mission-critical business and cultural priorities that give them the most influence and impact. They may not even be aware of what those are! This drives how they spend their time, how they think about their job, and how they do that job. And just as important, the way they do their job is inconsistent with the culture and mores of your organization.

How managers can help their people is a book in itself. So, what we have provided is a primer: Some bullet points on how you can help your people excel and shine, to your benefit, and your organization's benefit. Most of what we are describing in this chapter can be summed up as "Coach more than supervise." Managers acting as coaches to their team members is first and foremost an act of respect, which engenders respect. It is a core behavior of a high-performing executive. It is how you help others evolve, using your confidence in them to bring out their best:

- The first step in improving others' influence and impact is finding out what their job really is supposed to be. If you take the time, you and your colleagues can tell them most of the information they need. Other information is best obtained by encouraging them to observe what people do, how they respond, who succeeds and who struggles. What are their essential priorities? Are they totally focused on those priorities? What do they need from their team? What does their team need from them?

- You can help by paving the way for them and by giving them the time, resources, and encouragement they will need to do this right.

- Help them know themselves better. For senior leaders, make sure they go through some type of formal development program. At a minimum, give them a 360° survey, so they understand how they are perceived by their team, their peers, and you. Consider personality assessment by a trained evaluator, so they understand their styles and preferences.

- Help them know the business. To ensure they understand what the organization is all about, give them access to documents, including the organization's mission, vision, and purpose, business strategies, cultural norms, and the like. It is surprising how few people pay attention to a public company's financial statements or attend to quarterly reports. This is one of the best ways to help them think about the larger goals and objectives.

- Help them know you. Think through your own role, review your mission, vision, and remit. Look hard at your own strengths and preferences for how you work with others. A critical question for them is what you really need from them to make you and the organization more successful. Give them a chance to probe you and observe you—accept the possibility that what you do may not always match what you say.

- Help them know their stakeholders. Make sure they know who their stakeholders are. Remember, for most people in management, stakeholders are the wide range of people who talk to them, listen to them, supply them, benefit from them, and rely on them. Ensure your people understand what is really important to their stakeholders.

- Clarify what success looks like. What will the outcome be when they achieve their mission? Imagine yourself taking them out for a celebratory dinner two years in and saying "I am so proud of the way you have delivered on your work. You have influenced others throughout the organization, and several people have commented to me on your impact." What did they do?

- Be clear about the job. Make sure your people understand the deliverables, including general objectives and more specific goals and outcomes—their impact on you and the team. Separate this from the compensation process. Make sure they know what you need and expect. You may not have been as clear as you could be about your expectations. And, they may not have been listening as well as they could have. You may need to have these discussions with your team, or with an individual, more than once.

- Authority, responsibility, and accountability (ARA) are the critical elements of a manager–team member relationship. You grant them authority to do what is needed. They have to take responsibility for the work. And both of you deal with accountability. You hold them accountable; they embrace accountability. You own the strategy, and set the strategic guidelines. They own the execution of those strategies. The clearer your team members are, the more freedom they have to exercise their authority within those guidelines. Help them understand what operational and tactical decisions they are going to make in line with your strategic guidance.

- Leaders inspire and enable others to do their absolute best together to realize a meaningful and rewarding shared purpose. Great leaders bring out others' self-confidence in the process by emphasizing confidence-building in their approach to the direction, authority, resource, and accountability aspects of delegation.[i]

- Create psychological safety in your organization. It is essential that your people be able to influence you, and have an impact on what you do and think. If they cannot question you or give you feedback, how could they possibly influence anyone else? Amy Edmundson describes psychological safety as "a climate in which people are comfortable expressing and being themselves. . .when people have psychological safety at work, they feel comfortable sharing concerns and mistakes without fear of embarrassment or retribution. They are confident that they can speak up and won't be humiliated, ignored, or blamed."[ii]

- Building trust with your people is particularly important; without it, you are never sure if you and they are focused on the same things, with the same goals and objectives. Trust is built on the little things you do multiple times a day. For example, sarcasm undermines trust. Why? Because sarcasm is inherently aggressive, and when you are in a power relationship, sarcasm is hard to interpret. Do they mean it? Are they joking?

  > One executive, when discussing a high-priority project, said to a long-time team member, "I need this by end of day Friday." Andy replied, "What happens if I can't get it to you until Monday?" The leader said, dead-pan, "Then don't bother to come in." For a couple seconds, a flash of pure fear ran across Andy's face. Then the executive laughed, and the whole team laughed, except Andy, who just breathed a sigh of relief. Andy knew his boss well, but even in that context, he had a moment where he felt vulnerable.

- Don't micromanage. When you micromanage, you are reneging on your commitment to grant people authority. Managers micromanage for a variety of reasons. Some do not trust their people; some do not want to see people fail. Whatever the reason, micromanaging creates a negative spiral that demoralizes your people and guarantees you will, at some point, become overwhelmed. Your people, and hence you, will never be able to have the impact you want them to have if you are always fixing what they do.

- Show micro-interest. It is important for managers to understand the details of what their people are doing, even if they are consistently exceeding expectations. When you show interest in the details, you create opportunities for learning and growth, and create opportunities to provide positive feedback. And you demonstrate that you care about their work.

- Challenge them to do more than they think they can do.

- Help them evaluate their options and craft their go-forward plan to grow their influence and impact. Ensure they know:
  - The real mission (why) and vision (what)
  - Stakeholder and their priorities
  - Objectives/goals/outcomes
  - Top priorities in achieving those objectives/goals/outcomes
  - Action steps in line with those priorities
  - Personal changes to attitudes, relationships, and/or behaviors required and plans and resources to support those (technical, interpersonal/political, mental models, and managing emotions)
  - Milestones and timelines

- Work with them to compare their real strengths to the strengths required for success in the role. If the differences are minor and manageable, help them realize that and make adjustments. If the differences are complementary, make sure they know that you believe the differences are complementary through your words and actions. If the differences are mission-crippling, find ways to mitigate those issues.
- If the differences are insurmountable, collaborate to find a new path either inside or outside the organization. Sometimes it is not in anyone's best interest for your employee to continue working for you. How you support that decision can make a massive difference in how the story ends for your employee, your organization, and for you.
  - Focus on the strengths they do have and help them think through where those strengths can be better applied.
  - Help them think through what motivates them, and find other opportunities where they can experience that.
  - Help them consider their own preferences across behaviors, relationships, attitudes, values, and environment, and look for places where the culture more closely aligns with those.

Remember that leaders and managers succeed when their people are engaged, empowered, and focused. Helping your team members develop their influence and impact is the best way for you to expand your own influence and impact. The time devoted to helping them will return your investment multiple times over.

End Notes

i Bradt, G. (2019, November 5). How Great Leaders Bring Out Others' Self-Confidence. Forbes. Retrieved February 7, 2021 from https://www.forbes.com/sites/georgebradt/2019/11/05/how-great-leaders-bring-out-others-self-confidence/?sh=4b36d815422c

ii Edmundson, A. (2019). *The fearless organization: Creating psychological safety in the workplace for learning, innovation and growth.* (p. xvi). New York: John Wiley & Sons.

About the Authors

Bill Berman

Bill founded and leads Berman Leadership Development, a boutique consultancy based in New York City that advises executives and their teams from multiple industries. He is a business psychologist with more than 30 years' experience as an executive coach, senior line manager, clinician, and academic. Bill and his colleagues work with people from emerging leaders to C-suite executives, in a range of industries including financial services, pharmaceuticals, consumer products, professional services, technology, and manufacturing.

Before becoming a coach, Bill started his own software company in 1993 to track healthcare outcomes. In 2000, he sold the company to an enterprise healthcare information management system, where he served on the executive management team and had P&L responsibility for the professional services division until 2004. Bill's early career included both clinical work and faculty positions at Cornell University Medical College and at Fordham University, where he received tenure in 1994.

Bill received his B.A. from Harvard College, and his Ph.D. from Yale University. He is licensed in NY and CT, is a fellow of the American Psychological Association, and board certified by the American College of Professional Psychology. He is a past president of the Society of Consulting Psychology.

George Bradt

George has led the revolution in how people start new jobs—accelerating transitions so leaders and their teams reduce their rates of failure and fulfill potential. After Harvard and Wharton (MBA), he progressed through sales, marketing, and general management roles around the world at Procter & Gamble, Coca-Cola, and J.D. Power's Power Information Network spin-off as chief executive. Now he is chairman of PrimeGenesis, author of 10 books on onboarding and leadership, over 700 columns for Forbes, and 17 plays and musicals (book, lyrics, and music).

Other leadership and onboarding books by George:

- *The New Leader's 100-Day Action Plan* (Wiley, 4 editions, 2006–2016)
- *Onboarding: How to Get Your New Employees Up to Speed in Half the Time* (Wiley, 2009)
- *The Total Onboarding Program: An Integrated Approach* (Wiley/Pfeiffer, 2010)
- *First-Time Leader* (Wiley, 2014)
- *The New Job 100 Day Plan* (GHP Press, 2012)
- *Point of Inflection* (GHP Press, 2019)
- *CEO Boot Camp* (GHP Press, 2019)
- *The New Leader's Playbook* (GHP Press, one volume each year 2011–2020)
- *Executive Onboarding* (GHP Press, four volumes, 2020)

Guest Contributors

Greg Pennington, Ph.D.—Managing Partner at Pennpoint Consulting Group, LLC

Greg has more than 30 years' experience increasing organizational capability through executive coaching, team effectiveness, and leadership development programs and presentations. Prior to starting his coaching practice, Greg served as vice president of Senior Leader Development and Planning for Johnson Controls, Leadership & Talent Practice Leader, The Hay Group, and Senior Consultant, RHR International. He has worked in both internal and external roles in human resources, training and development, diversity and inclusion, and executive coaching. Greg earned his BA in psychology from Harvard College, and his Ph.D. in psychology from the University of North Carolina—Chapel Hill.

Kerry Bessey—Chief Human Resources Officer, Memorial Sloan Kettering Cancer Center

Ben Dattner, Ph.D.—Executive Coach, Organizational Psychologist; Founding Principal, Dattner Consulting, LLC

Leo F. Flanagan, Jr., Ph.D.—Principal Research Fellow, The Conference Board; Founder, The Center for Resilience

Joe Garbus—Chief Talent and Inclusion Officer at Marsh & Co.

Carol Kauffman, Ph.D., ABPP—Founder, Institute of Coaching, Harvard Medical School

Aithan Shapira, MFA, Ph.D.—Pianist, painter, and lecturer at MIT; Founder of Tilt

Hy Pomerance, Ph.D.—Chief Talent Officer at Cleary Gottlieb Steen & Hamilton LLP

Erica L. Spencer, Ph.D.—Vice President, Global Learning and Development, Marriott International

Barry Schub—Former Chief Human Resources Officer, New York Life Insurance

References

Abdel-Raheem, A. (2020). "Mental model theory as a model for analysing visual and multimodal discourse." *Journal of Pragmatics*, 155: 303–320.

Allen, R. (April 26, 2011). When Reagan Was Shot, Who Was "in Control" at the White House? Washington Post. Retrieved February 7, 2021 from https://www.washingtonpost.com/opinions/when-reagan-was-shot-who-was-in-control-at-the-white-house/2011/03/23/AFJlrfYB_story.html

American Factory. (2019). Streamed. Netflix.

Bandura, A. (2001). "Social cognitive theory: An agentic perspective." *Annual Review of Psychology*, 52:1: 1–26.

Bennis, W., & Nanus, B. (1985). *Leaders: the strategies for taking charge* (p. 41). NY: Harper & Row.

Bolles, R. (2019). *What color is your parachute? 2020: A practical manual for job-hunters and career-changers*, Revised. Berkeley, CA: Ten Speed Press.

Bongers, A., Northoff, G., & Flynn, A. B. (2019). "Working with mental models to learn and visualize a new reaction mechanism." *Chemistry Education Research and Practice*, 20(3): 554–569.

Bourke, J., and Titus, A. (2019). "Why inclusive leaders are good for organizations, and how to become one." Harvard Business Review. Retrieved February 7, 2021 from https://hbr.org/2019/03/why-inclusive-leaders-are-good-for-organizations-and-how-to-become-one

Boyatzis, R. E., Goleman, D., & Rhee, K. (2000). "Clustering competence in emotional intelligence: Insights from the Emotional Competence Inventory (ECI)." *Handbook of Emotional Intelligence*, 99(6): 343–362.

Bradt, G. (October, 2020). How Naming Jane Fraser CEO Advances Citibank's Client Focus. Forbes. Retrieved February 7, 2021 from https://www.forbes.com/sites/georgebradt/2020/09/10/how-naming-jane-fraser-ceo-advances-citibanks-client-focus/?sh=2282e4f21e97

Bradt, G. (April, 2011). Be Like Zappo's Tony Hsieh: Answer Three Key Onboarding Due Diligence Questions. Forbes. Retrieved February 7, 2021 from https://www.forbes.com/sites/georgebradt/2011/08/10/be-like-zappos-tony-hsieh-answer-three-key-onboarding-due-diligence-questions/?sh=404ddffeb5bb

Bradt, G. (February 16, 2016). Accountability: The Essential Link Between Empowerment And Engagement. Forbes. Retrieved February 7, 2021 from https://www.forbes.com/sites/georgebradt/2016/02/16/accountability-the-essential-link-between-empowerment-and-engagement/#5e690ffc2a4a

Bradt, G. (July 7, 2020). The Difference Between Deputies and Chiefs of Staff. Forbes. Retrieved February 7, 2021 from https://www.forbes.com/sites/georgebradt/2020/07/07/the-difference-between-deputies-and-chiefs-of-staff/#37532032119f

Bradt, G. (November 27, 2018). The Secret Sauce in a Best Current Thinking Approach to Problem-Solving. Forbes. Retrieved February 7, 2021 from https://www.forbes.com/sites/georgebradt/2018/11/27/the-secret-sauce-in-a-best-current-thinking-approach-to-problem-solving/?sh=50ebdda56b34

Bradt, G. (April 27, 2011). The Importance of Due Diligence Before Accepting a Job. *PrimeGenesis*. Retrieved February 7, 2021 from www.primegenesis.com/our-blog/2011/04/the-importance-of-due-diligence-before-accepting-a-job

Bradt, G. (April, 2011). Top Executive Recruiters Agree There Are Only Three True Job Interview Questions. Forbes. Retrieved February 7, 2021 from https://www.forbes.com/sites/georgebradt/2011/04/27/top-executive-recruiters-agree-there-are-only-three-key-job-interview-questions/?sh=4b632096f35c

Bradt, G. (July, 2012). Give Your Boss What She Needs, Not Just What She Requests. Forbes. Retrieved February 7, 2021 from https://www.forbes.com/sites/georgebradt/2012/07/25/give-your-boss-what-she-needs-not-just-what-she-requests/?sh=555b09376a8f

Bradt, G. (August, 2013). What VW's Next CEO Must Do To Save The Organization. Forbes. Retrieved February 7, 2021 from https://www.forbes.com/sites/georgebradt/2015/09/23/what-vws-next-ceo-must-do-to-save-the-organization/?sh=35e20a7e7d55

Bradt, G. (November, 2013). Why You Don't Get To Choose Your Mission. It Chooses You. Forbes. Retrieved February 7, 2021 from https://www.forbes.com/sites/georgebradt/2013/11/26/why-you-dont-get-to-choose-your-mission-it-chooses-you/?sh=3016a43a221b

Bradt, G. (September, 2015). How Leaders Can Address The Elephant(s) In The Room. Forbes. Retrieved February 7, 2021 from https://www.forbes.com/sites/georgebradt/2013/08/07/how-leaders-can-address-the-elephants-in-the-room/?sh=4513bcec5660

Bradt, G. (October, 2019). As an Executive Onboarding into a New Role, Engage Intellectually, Emotionally and Practically—in That Order. Forbes. Retrieved February 7, 2021 from https://www.forbes.com/sites/georgebradt/2019/10/22/as-an-executive-onboarding-into-a-new-role-engage-intellectually-emotionally-and-practically--in-that-order/?sh=58d89f9d5be6

Bradt, G. (November, 2019). How Great Leaders Bring Out Others' Self-Confidence. Forbes. Retrieved February 7, 2021 from https://www.forbes.com/sites/georgebradt/2019/11/05/how-great-leaders-bring-out-others-self-confidence/sss?sh=21955544422c

Bradt, G. B., Check, J. A., & Lawler, J. A. (2016) *The new leader's 100 day action plan* (4th ed.). Hoboken, NJ: John Wiley & Sons.

Breaugh, J. A. (2017). The contribution of job analysis to recruitment. (pp. 12–28). *The Wiley Blackwell handbook of the psychology of recruitment, selection and employee retention.* Hoboken, NJ: John Wiley & Sons.

Briggs, K. C. (1987). *Myers-Briggs type indicator: Form G.* Palo Alto, CA: Consulting Psychologists Press.

Briley, D. A., & Tucker-Drob, E. M. (2017). "Comparing the developmental genetics of cognition and personality over the life span." *Journal of Personality*, 85(1): 51–64.

Cattell, H. E. P., & Mead, A. D. (2008). The sixteen personality factor questionnaire *(16PF)*. In Boyle, G. J., Matthews, G., & Saklofske, D. H. (eds), *The Sage handbook of personality theory and assessment, vol. 2: Personality measurement and testing,* (pp. 135–159). Sage Publications, Inc.

Cleveland, S., & Cleveland, M. (2020). Toward Leadership Agility. In Merviö, M., *Global Issues and Innovative Solutions in Healthcare, Culture, and the Environment,* (pp. 1–13). Hershey, PA: IGI Global.

Cleveland, M., & Cleveland, S. (2020). "Culturally agile leadership: A relational leadership development approach." *International Journal of Public and Private Perspectives on Healthcare, Culture, and the Environment* (IJPP-PHCE), 4(1): 1–9.

Cohen, G. R. (2009). *Just ask leadership: Why great managers always ask the right questions.* NY: McGraw-Hill.

Collins, J. (2001). *Good to great: Why some companies make the leap and others don't.* NY: HarperCollins Publishers, Inc.

Cooley, C. H. (1992). *Human nature and the social order.* Piscataway, NJ: Transaction Publishers.

Covey, S. R., & Covey, S. (2020). *The 7 habits of highly effective people.* New York, NY: Simon & Schuster.

De Meuse, K. P., Dai G., & Hallenbeck, G. S. (2010). "Learning agility: A construct whose time has come." *Consulting Psychology Journal: Practice and Research*, 62(2): 119.

Dennis, P. (2006). *Getting the right things done: a leader's guide to planning and execution.* Boston, MA: Lean Enterprise Institute.

DeRue, D. Scott, Susan J. Ashford, and Christopher G. Myers. "Learning agility: In search of conceptual clarity and theoretical grounding." *Industrial and Organizational* Psychology 5, no. 3 (2012): 258–279.

De Vries, M. F. "Coaching the toxic leader." *Harvard Business Review* 92, no. 4 (2014): 100.

DiClemente, Carlo C., and Mary Marden Velasquez. "Motivational interviewing and the stages of change." *Motivational interviewing: Preparing people for change* 2 (2002): 201–216.

Doran, George T. "There's a SMART way to write management's goals and objectives." *Management review* 70, no. 11 (1981): 35–36.

Edmondson, A. C. (2018). *The fearless organization: Creating psychological safety in the workplace for learning, innovation, and growth.* Hoboken, NJ: John Wiley & Sons.

Eichinger, R. W., & Lombardo, M. M. (2004). "Learning agility as a prime indicator of potential." *People and Strategy*, 27(4): 12.

Epton, T., Currie S., & Armitage, C. J. (2017). "Unique effects of setting goals on behavior change: Systematic review and meta-analysis." *Journal of Consulting and Clinical Psychology*, 85(12): 1182.

Felipe, C. M., José L. R., & Leal-Rodríguez, A. L. (2017). "Impact of organizational culture values on organizational agility." *Sustainability*, 9(12): 2354.

Ferdeli, Z., Wagiarto H., & Hakim, L. (2020). "Effect of Employee Empowerment And Integrity on Company Performance Through Organizational Commitments as a Mediation Variables On Pt. TGI Company." *IAR Journal of Humanities and Social Science*, 1(3).

Ferdman, B. M., Prime, J., & Riggio, R. E. (eds) (2019). *Inclusive leadership.* Milton Park, UK: Routledge.

Flanigan, M. S. (2016). "Diagnosing and changing organizational culture in strategic enrollment management." *Strategic Enrollment Management Quarterly*, 4(3): 117–129.

Flaum, J. P., & Winkler, B. (June 8, 2015). "Improve your ability to learn." Harvard Business Review (online). Retrieved February 7, 2021 from https://hbr.org/2015/06/improve-your-ability-to-learn.

Fleenor, J. W., Taylor, S., & Chappelow, C. (2020). *Leveraging the impact of 360-degree feedback.* Oakland, CA: Berrett-Koehler Publishers, Inc.

Forester, J., & McKibbon, G. (2020). "Beyond blame: leadership, collaboration and compassion in the time of COVID-19." *Socio-Ecological Practice Research*, 2(3): 205–216.

Frank, C. J., & Magnone, P. F. (2011). *Drinking from a fire hose: Making smarter decisions without drowning in information.* NY: Portfolio.

Frazier, M. L., Fainshmidt, S., Klinger, R. L., Pezeshkan, A., & Vracheva, V. (2017). "Psychological safety: A meta-analytic review and extension." *Personnel Psychology*, 70(1): 113–165.

Gabriel, Y., Gray, D. E., & Goregaokar, H. (2013). "Job loss and its aftermath among managers and professionals: Wounded, fragmented and flexible." *Work, Employment and Society*, 27(1): 56–72.

Gebelein, S. H. (1999). *The successful executive's handbook: Development suggestions for today's executives.* Minneapolis, MN: Personnel Decisions International.

Gebelein, S. H., Nelson-Neuhaus, K. J., Skube, C. J., Lee, D. G., Stevens, L. A., Hellervik, L. W., & Davis, B. L. (2010). *Successful Manager's Handbook.* Minneapolis, MN: Personnel Decisions International

Goleman, D., Boyatzis, R. E., & McKee, A. (2013). *Primal leadership: Unleashing the power of emotional intelligence.* Cambridge, MA: Harvard Business Press.

Gong, Y., Wang, M., Huang, J-C., & S. Y. Cheung. (2017). "Toward a goal orientation–based feedback-seeking typology: Implications for employee performance outcomes." *Journal of Management*, 43(4): 1234–1260.

Gould, L. J. (2018). *The systems psychodynamics of organizations: Integrating the group relations approach, psychoanalytic, and open systems perspectives.* Milton Park, UK: Routledge.

Gustafsson, H., Lundqvist, C. C., & Tod, D. (2017). "Cognitive behavioral intervention in sport psychology: A case illustration of the exposure method with an elite athlete." *Journal of Sport Psychology in Action*, 8(3): 152–162.

Han, S. J., & Stieha, V. (2020). "Growth mindset for human resource development: A scoping review of the literature with recommended interventions." *Human Resource Development Review*, 19(3): 309–331.

Hogan, K. (2010). *The science of influence: How to get anyone to say "yes" in 8 minutes or less!* Hoboken, NJ: John Wiley & Sons.

Hogan, R. (2020). "How to build Hogan assessment systems." *Consulting Psychology Journal: Practice and Research*, 72(1): 50.

Joseph, T. M. (2011). "The psychological contract: What is missing? What is next?" *Journal of Psychological Issues in Organizational Culture*, 2(1): 67–75.

Kahneman, D. (2011). *Thinking, fast and slow.* New York, NY: Macmillan.

Kaplan, B., & Kaiser, R. (2006). *The versatile leader: Make the most of your strengths without overdoing it,* (Vol. 309). Hoboken, NJ: John Wiley & Sons.

Kaul, A. (2019). "Culture vs strategy: Which to precede, which to align?" *Journal of Strategy and Management*, 12 (1), 116-136.

Keegan, R., & Lahey, L. (2009). *Immunity to change: How to overcome it and unlock the potential in yourself and your organization.* Cambridge, MA: Harvard University Press.

Korn Ferry Institute. (2017). The Black P&L Leader: Insights and Lessons from Senior Black P&L Leaders in the United States. Retrieved February 7, 2021 from https://www.kornferry.com/content/dam/kornferry/docs/pdfs/korn-ferry_ theblack-pl-leader.pdf

Kshatriya, S. (2016). "Job Analysis and its Positive Impact on key Recruitment and Selection Processes: A Case Study." *Al Dar Research Journal for Sustainability*, 1(1): 46–68.

Lawler, J., & Bilson, A. (2009). *Social work management and leadership: Managing complexity with creativity. Milton Park*, UK: Routledge.

Leary, M. R., & Tangney, J. P. (eds) (2011). *Handbook of self and identity*. New York, NY: Guilford Press.

Levinson, D. J. (1978). *The seasons of a man's life*. New York, NY: Random House Digital, Inc.

Maciejewski, P. K., Zhang, B., Block, S. D., & Prigerson, H. G. (2007). "An empirical examination of the stage theory of grief." *Journal of the American Medical Association*, 297(7): 716–723.

Maddux, J. E., & Gosselin, J. T. (2012). Self-efficacy. In Leary, M. R., & Tangney, J. P. (eds), *Handbook of self and identity*, (pp. 198–224). New York, NY: The Guilford Press.

Maslow, A. (1943). "A theory of human motivation." *Psychological Review*, 50(4): 370–396.

Masters, B. (March 30, 2009). "Rise of a headhunter." Financial Times. Retrieved February 7, 2021 from https://www.ft.com/content/19975256-1af2-11de-8aa3-0000779fd2ac

Maurer, R. (December 12, 2018). Why Are Workers Quitting Their Jobs in Record Numbers? Society of Human Resources Management (SHRM. org). Retrieved February 7, 2021 from https://www.shrm.org/resourcesand tools/hr-topics/talent-acquisition/pages/workers-are-quitting-jobs-record-numbers.aspx

Mead, G. H. (1962). *Mind, self, and society*. Chicago: University of Chicago.

Mehrabian, A. (1981). *Silent messages: Implicit communication of emotions and attitudes*. Belmont, CA: Wadsworth.

Menard, P., Warkentin, M., & Lowry, P. B. (2018). "The impact of collectivism and psychological ownership on protection motivation: A cross-cultural examination." *Computers & Security*, 75: 147–166.

Meyer, E. (2014). *The culture map*. NY: Public Affairs.

Miller, L. & Jackson, B. (2007). *UP influence, power and the U perspective: The art of getting what you want* (1st ed.). New York, NY: Your Career Doctors Press.

Mosanya, M. (2019). "Exploring cultural intelligence relationships with growth mindset, grit, coping and academic stress in the United Arab Emirates." *Middle East Journal of Positive Psychology*, 5(1): 42–59.

Mosanya, M. (2020). "Buffering academic stress during the COVID-19 pandemic related social isolation: Grit and growth mindset as protective factors against the impact of loneliness." *International Journal of Applied Positive Psychology*, 5(3): 1–16.

Neimeyer, R. A. (2001). "Meaning reconstruction & the experience of loss." *American Psychological Association.*

Neubert, M. J., Hunter, E. M., & Tolentino, R. C. (2016). "A servant leader and their stakeholders: When does organizational structure enhance a leader's influence?" *The Leadership Quarterly*, 27(6): 896–910.

Owen, J. E., Mahatmya, D., & Carter, R. (2017). Dominance, influence, steadiness, and conscientiousness (DISC) assessment tool. In *Encyclopedia of personality and individual differences*. (Vol. 10, pp. 978–973). Cham, Switzerland: Springer.

Paoletti, J., Reyes, D. L., & Salas, E. (2019). Leaders, teams, and their mental models. In Mumford, M. D., & Higgs, C. A. (eds), *Leader thinking skills: Capacities for contemporary leadership*, (pp. 277–306). London: Taylor & Francis.

Papa, A., & Lancaster, N. (2016). "Identity continuity and loss after death, divorce, and job loss." *Self and Identity*, 15(1): 47–61.

Poe, L. F., Brooks, N. G., Korzaan, M., Hulshult, A. R., & Woods, D. M. (2020). "Promoting positive student outcomes: The use of reflection and planning activities with a growth-mindset focus and SMART goals." In *Proceedings of the EDSIG Conference ISSN*, Vol. 2473, p. 4901.

Prewett, M. S., Tett, R. P., & Christiansen, N. D. (2013). A review and comparison of 12 personality inventories on key psychometric characteristics. In Christiansen N. D., & Tett, R. P. *Handbook of personality at work*, (pp. 191–225). London: Routledge.

Prigerson, H. G., & Maciejewski, P. K. (2008). "Grief and acceptance as opposite sides of the same coin: Setting a research agenda to study peaceful acceptance of loss." *The British Journal of Psychiatry*, 193(6): 435–437.

Reina, C. S., Kristie M. R., Peterson, S. J., Byron, K. & Hom, P. W. (2018). "Quitting the boss? The role of manager influences tactics and employee emotional engagement in voluntary turnover." *Journal of Leadership & Organizational Studies*, 25: 5–18.

Rock, David. (2008). "SCARF: A brain-based model for collaborating with and influencing others." *NeuroLeadership Journal*, 1(1): 44–52.

Ross, Lee. The intuitive psychologist and his shortcomings: Distortions in the attribution process. In Zeigler-Hill, V., & Shackelford, T. (eds), *Advances in experimental social psychology*, (Vol. 10, pp. 173–220). NY: Academic Press.

Rousseau, D. M., Hansen, S. D., & M. Tomprou. (2018). "A dynamic phase model of psychological contract processes." *Journal of Organizational Behavior*, 39(9): 1081–1098.

Schank, R., and Abelson, R. P. (1977). *Scripts, plans, goals and understanding: An inquiry into human knowledge structures*. Hillsdale, NJ: Lawrence Erlbaum Associates.

Schein, E. H. (1992). Defining organizational culture. In Shafritz, J. M., Ott, J. S., and Jang, Y. S. *Classics of organization theory*, (Vol. 3, pp. 490–502). Pacific Grove, CA: Brooks/Cole.

Schein, E. H. (2004). *Organizational culture and leadership*, 3rd Ed. San Francisco, CA: JosseyBass.

Schmidtke, J. M., and Cummings, A. (2017). "The effects of virtualness on teamwork behavioral components: The role of shared mental models." *Human Resource Management Review*, 27(4): 660–677.

Shannon, E. (Sept 23, 2015). How Two Dogged Clean Air Sleuths Exposed Massive VW Deceit. Environmental Working Group. Retrieved February 7, 2021 from https://www.ewg.org/enviroblog/2015/09/how-two-dogged-clear-air-sleuths-exposed-massive-vw-deceit

Sharma, S., and Sarraf, R. (2018). "Significance of Herrmann brain dominance instrument' (hbdi) for organizational development." *Advance and Innovative Research*, 5(1): 95.

Sheehy, G. (2011). *New passages: Mapping your life across time*. New York, NY: Ballantine Books.

Sinek, S. (September, 2009). How Great Leaders Inspire Action. TED Talks. Retrieved February 7, 2021 from https://www.ted.com/talks/simon_sinek_how_great_leaders_inspire_action?language=en

Struijs, S. Y., Lamers, F., Verdam, M. G. E., van Ballegooijen, W., Spinhoven, P., van der Does, W., & Penninx, B. W. J. H. (2020). "Temporal stability of symptoms of affective disorders, cognitive vulnerability and personality over time." *Journal of Affective Disorders*, 260: 77–83.

Taylor, S. E. (1991). "Asymmetrical effects of positive and negative events: The mobilization-minimization hypothesis." *Psychological Bulletin*, 110(1): 67–85.

Teece, D. J. (2018). "Dynamic capabilities as (workable) management systems theory." *Journal of Management & Organization*, 24(3): 359–368.

Thornton, M. A., & Tamir, D. I. (2017). Mental models accurately predict emotion transitions. *Proceedings of the National Academy of Sciences*, 114(23): 5982–5987.

Thurlings, M., Vermeulen, M., Bastiaens, T., & Stijnen, S. (2013). "Understanding feedback: A learning theory perspective." *Educational Research Review*, 9: 1–15.

Vandaveer, V. V., Lowman, R. L., Pearlman, K., & Brannick, J. P. (2016). "A practice analysis of coaching psychology: Toward a foundational competency model." *Consulting Psychology Journal: Practice and Research*, 68(2): 118.

Van Velsor, E., McCauley, C. D., & Ruderman, M. N. (eds) (2010). (Vol. 122). *The center for creative leadership handbook of leadership development.* Hoboken, NJ: John Wiley & Sons.

Vosse, B. J. F., & Aliyu, O. A. (2018). "Determinants of employee trust during organisational change in higher institutions." *Journal of Organizational Change Management*, 31: 1105–1118.

Warrick, D. D. (2017). "What leaders need to know about organizational culture." *Business Horizons*, 60(3): 395–404.

Index